The Formula of Concord

Core and Highlights

The Doctrine of Election

in

Questions and Answers

*The Formula of Concord - Core and Highlights &
The Doctrine of Election in Questions and Answers*

Copyright 2012 © Lutheran News, Inc. All Rights Reserved.
No portion of this book may be reproduced in any form, except for quotations in reviews, articles, and speeches, without permission from the publisher.

**Library of Congress Card
Lutheran News, Inc.
684 Luther Lane
New Haven, Mo 63068
Published 2012
Printed in the United States of America,
Lightning Source Inc., La Vergne, TN
ISBN #978-0-9644799-4-4**

The Formula of Concord

Core and Highlights

With a historical introduction and
accompanied by short explanatory comments

To the Lutheran Christian people

Presented at the request of the worthy Evangelical Lutheran Conference of
North America

By
C. F. W. Walther

Translated by
Kenneth Howes

Translator's Preface

As we approach the 200th anniversary of Carl Walther's birth, it is right that we take a closer look at his many works. This titan of American Lutheranism wrote an enormous volume of work, less than half of which has ever been translated into English. That is largely the result of the very sudden and swift abandonment of German by the Lutheran Church-Missouri Synod in the 1940's. At the beginning of that decade, most of the theological work of the synod was still carried on in German, and most of its churches still held their services in German; by its end, everything was in English. By the end of the 1950's, German in our churches was for the most part only a memory, and by the mid-1970's, it was barely that.

This book, intended primarily for laymen as an explanation of the Formula of Concord, is one that should long since have been translated and placed in the hands of the laity. Today's American Lutheran laymen are almost entirely unaware of the scope of the Lutheran Confessions and their contents. They are taught the Small Catechism—if they are taught that; there are alarming stories of churches that do not even use that—before confirmation. There is not another presentation of the Lutheran Confessions thereafter. They may have heard of the Augsburg Confession, especially if the full name of their church ends with the letters "UAC" and they have been told what those letters mean; most have not.

The result is that most of their ideas about religion are formed not by Lutherans but by television preachers and popular books. As a pastor of my acquaintance remarked a few years ago, most have been taught less by Martin Luther than by Billy Graham. The result is that in America, the typical Lutheran's beliefs could be described as those of a Baptist who believes in the Real Presence in the Communion. Even infant baptism is sometimes postponed "until they can reach their own decision." At least one Missouri Synod church has done "consecrations" instead of baptizing a number of small children.

Some of the reasons for this are not entirely in the control of pastors and lay elders who are concerned about this development. In an era of "Chreasters" who come to church twice a year, most of the preaching they hear is that of Southern Baptist or even Pentecostal televangelists, and most of the religious literature they read, if any, is the material sold in "Christian bookstores"—again, most of it Baptist or Pentecostal.

Our pastors and lay leaders are not without blame, though. How many pastors are using instructional materials by Baptist writers? How many elders are themselves products of hearing Baptist—or worse—preachers on the television? How many pastors, music directors and music committees have selected "contemporary" music for their services, songs of Methodist, Baptist and Pentecostal provenance that carry their Arminian theology of decision and subjective view of God? How many, contrary to the clear position of the Missouri Synod, participate in joint services with congregations of the Church of the Nazarene, United Methodist Church and other similar bodies, at which the teachings of those churches are mixed with ours?

The fault lies not only with liberal or unionist pastors. There is another sort of pastor, generally found in the supposedly confessional camp, that does not believe that laymen should read their Bibles except under the closest supervision of a pastor—that if they read the Bible on their own, that leads to "private interpretation." They take the view that the Small Catechism is all that the layman needs to know on his own—everything else that he is to think and to know, the pastor will tell him from the pulpit. In that perspective, a full familiarity of laymen with all the confessions becomes unnecessary, perhaps even undesirable.

Walther would have rejected the views of both of these camps energetically. He, with the Reformers and the orthodox dogmaticians, emphasized the need for full understanding by laymen of what was taught and believed. To that end, he wrote this book, which is a summary of the Epitome of the Formula of Concord, with a historical background.

This translation is submitted that today's laymen may understand the Formula of Concord, an essential part of our confessions, and that pastors have a vehicle with which to explain it to them. Where I believe it would be helpful, I have added footnotes explaining matters that, though they should already be well-known to pastors, are probably unfamiliar to the lay reader. It should be remembered that this is essentially a pastoral, not an academic, document. There are no footnotes in the usual sense by Walther, and the source of many of his quotations is omitted. There is, however, no reason to doubt the authenticity of any of his quotations, Walther having been a very thorough scholar as can be seen in his other works.

To preserve the exact sense of the text, Bible quotations are generally my translations of Walther's German. Any citations to Luther's Bible are to the 1534 edition, which was reprinted in facsimile a few years ago.[1] In the section on the Formula of Concord, the translation of the Formula is this translator's own; the translation appearing in the *Concordia Triglotta*[2] was used for comparison purposes only in checking the translator's results.

Soli Deo gloria!
Chicago, February 27, 2008   Kenneth Howes

---

[1] Martin Luther, tr. and ed., *Biblia Sacra*, 1534 ed. in facsimile (Köln: Taschen, 2003).

[2] The 3-language (German, Latin, English) edition of the *Book of Concord* originally published by Concordia Publishing House in 1921, and reprinted by Northwestern Publishing House in 1978.

Foreword

Already in the year 1663, the old, faithful theologian in Rostock[3], Johannes Quistorp, complains in a writing entitled "Pious Wishes", as follows: We are all called relatives of the Augsburg Confession, but in our lands this public confession of faith is pushed neither publicly nor privately with the youth, just as if it had come to light only for the sake of the learned."

All true watchmen on the rooftops of our Lutheran Zion have had, sadly, to agree with this complaint up to the present day. Thousands and thousands have called themselves Lutherans, and call themselves Lutherans, who are completely unacquainted even with the Augsburg Confession. This lack of familiarity with the basic general confession and even more with the other public confessional writings of our church[4] has had the sad consequence that false teachers have been able to push their way in from every direction into our church, so that our Lutheran people has allowed itself to be pastored by these false teachers as its shepherds, and that, without serious resistance in the congregations, the old pure church and school books have been done away with, and in their place, all kinds of falsified, even openly Godless, rationalistic books of this kind, agendas, catechisms, reading books, etc., have been introduced.

If our Lutheran people were familiar with and directed to the Confessions of our church, and accustomed to test the teaching of their preachers and the writings to be introduced into church and school according to them, our church would never have fallen into the dreadful state of collapse in which it finds itself, namely in our old German fatherland. Then our Lutheran people would no longer be taught the abominable heresies that are now being taught orally and in writing and are sold as Lutheran teachings. Even the simplest would really then not have needed to dispute at length from the Scriptures, but everyone would have been able to say then: "Our church confesses this in its unaltered Augsburg Confession, it teaches this in its Smalcald Articles, it teaches this in its Formula of Concord, etc.. You have a sacred obligation to that as a Lutheran preacher or teacher; if you

---

[3] A port city on the Baltic in north central Germany, in what was for some forty years East Germany.

[4] In addition to the Augsburg Confessions, the confessional writings of the Lutheran Church are contained in the Book of Concord: the Apology of the Augsburg Confession, the Smalcald Articles, the Treatise on the Power and Primacy of the Pope, the Small Catechism, the Large Catechism, and the Epitome (short form) and Solid Declaration (long form) of the Formula of Concord. This book is principally concerned with the Epitome.

vary from that, if you teach otherwise, then I do not want to hear you, but rather, by the command of my Lord: 'Beware of the false prophets,' Matt. 7:15, flee from you as a false prophet."

As the day now arrives on the 29th of May of this year, 1877, on which once, exactly 300 years earlier, namely on May 29, 1577, the splendid final confession of our dear evangelical Lutheran Church, the so-called Formula of Concord, was completed in the Bergen Cloister near Magdeburg with God's grace and help, the worthy Evangelical Lutheran Synodical Conference of North America has commissioned the undersigned to provide for our dear Lutheran Christian people a reprinting of the first part[5] of the Formula of Concord, which contains its core and highlights, that is, a comprehensive summary, to accompany it with some comments necessary for explanation, and to put in front of it a historical introduction.

Unfortunately the undersigned was really not now able to give the diligence to the composition of this little book that the important subject of the same demands; but as there appeared to be no one else who wanted to undertake the work, and the three hundredth jubilee celebration of the Formula of Concord is already at the door, may the goodly reader take the little work of the undersigned indulgently, until others are moved by the great shortcomings of the same to make it better, who have more skill as well as more time for such a work.

For our Formula of Concord is truly worth it, that it unfurls as its so long-wrapped up banner of faith for our Lutheran Christian people, and that the treasures of Godly knowledge that are in this confession be shown to them. It is certainly without doubt, as it was called by orthodox teachers already 300 years ago, the last purely-sounding confessional trumpet of this last age.

The historical introduction at the beginning of the present little book on the Formula of Concord should not be considered a cohesive history of our Church from Luther's death to the completion of the Formula of Concord, but rather contains from this history only that which appeared necessary to be reported for a better understanding of the articles of the Formula of Concord. Everything reported is drawn from the most dependable sources, which, however, we have intentionally not named, for this book is not written for scholars but, as the title says, is for the Lutheran Christian people, namely for such Lutheran Christians as have a demand to learn to know the teaching of their church thoroughly, and for whom it is therefore only a desire and a joy not only to read, but, with diligence, to study with diligence the confessions of fatih and doctrine in their church.

The intention of the publisher of this little book in that regard has been this: that the Christian reader read the historical introduction contained in the first part first, and then that he read through, for each individual article of the Formula of Concord in the second part,

---

[5] Generally called the Epitome.

the chapter of the historical introduction belonging to that article one more time. By means of the index provided in the second part, he will find the applicable chapter easily. The book is not written for entertainment. A hasty leafing through will therefore be of little use. It is to be studied, with the proof-stone of the Word of God in hand. Hopefully no one will regard that as an excessive demand on Christians who are not preachers by profession. According to God's Word (Eph. 4:14; Heb. 5:12-14), those, too, who hold no teaching office in the Church, should not remain children in their knowledge, who let themselves be swayed and rocked back and forth with every wind of teaching, through the knavery of people and deception by which they sneak up on us to misdirect us, but become "masters", who by habit have practiced minds to distinguish good and evil.

Oh, that God would awaken ever more such Christians and equip those who are not content to have learned "the first letters of the divine Word" but prepare themselves for "the work of the Office," that "thereby the Body of Christ," that is, His holy Church, "is built up." For God wants to have such Christians, and the Church always, and especially now, has need of such Christians; namely, such mature Christians who just like the the Bereans take up the Word quite willingly, but hold no teaching for true just because their Herr Pastor taught them that, who seek no other master than Jesus Christ in true faith, and therefore search daily in the Scriptures to see whether what they hear and read also holds up (Acts 17:11), and in relation to all teachings of faith always ultimately say, as once that Samaritan to the Samaritan woman after she had announced Christ to them, "Now we believe, not because of thy saying: for we have heard him ourselves and know that this is indeed the Christ, the Savior of the world."[6]

Should the present little book help even a little to equip such Christians, then all the meager work directed to it has been worth it, and the publisher of the same would praise God highly, that He has made one entirely unworthy worthy by grace to have been His tool.

May the Christian reader, then, with regard to the last saying, because God's Word has gathered our Church in these last times, say of the dear Formula of Concord, with the undersigned, by David's precedent: "We boast that thou helpest us, and in the name of our God we raise up banners." (Ps. 20:5) (Luther)[7]

Amen! In Jesus' name! Amen!

St. Louis, Mo., in March, 1877.   C. F. W. Walther

---

[6]John 4:42.

[7]Walther, in the original, numbers this as Ps. 20:6; he apparently counted "A psalm of David" as verse 1.

Historical Introduction

First Chapter

Luther's Predictions, What Would Happen After His Death

It was on the day of Concord, February 18, 1546, that Luther died in peace in Eisleben, the town where he was born, in the doctrine that he had confessed in his life orally and in writing. With him also died the concord, that is, the unity, which had governed the evangelical Lutheran Church until his death. Hardly had he shut his eyes, division of every kind broke out over our Lutheran Zion in Germany like a horrible storm flood that overthrows everything.

Luther himself had not only sensed it but had predicted with clear words, informed by God's Word as well as by the history of the Church in all times and by his own experience. He had repeatedly expressed it, first really as his own conviction, that doctrine, when it comes to light somewhere in its apostolic purity, ordinarily remains pure only a short time, about as long as the life of a person. He writes as much in, for example, in his *Church Postils*,

> He (the Apostle Paul) demonstrates in 2 Cor. 6:1 the danger, in order that one not miss out on grace. He shows there with certainty that the preaching of the Gospel is not an eternal, lasting, remaining doctrine, but is like a moving cloudburst, that moves on; what it hits, it hits, what it misses, it misses; but it does not come again, and also does not remain in the same place, but rather the sun and the heat come afterward and dry it up.[8]
>
> Experience gives us that, too, that in no place in the world does the Gospel last longer than one man's thoughts; as long as those remained who brought it up, it remained and grew; when the same were gone, so was the light. Right away the divisive spirits and the false teachers followed. Thus Moses proclaims also in Deut. 31:29, that the children of Israel would spoil it after his death, as then the book of Judges also shows: as soon as a judge in whose time the Word of God emerged died, they fell away again and it went badly with them. And King Joash did right as long as the High Priest Jehoiada lived; after that, it was over.
>
> And after Christ and the time of the Apostles, the world became full of divisive spirits and false teachers, as St. Paul also announced and said, "For I know this, that after my departing shall grievous wolves enter in among you, not sparing the flock." (Acts 20:29) And so it is now, too: we have the Gospel fine and pure, and it is the time of grace or blessing, and a pleasant day; but soon hereafter it will be over. (St. L. XII:437-438; Walch XII:584-585)

In the Table Talk, there is, further, the following saying of Luther's: "As soon as 40 years are over, in which the Word of God has been preached purely, it's[9] stopped, and a great calamity ensued." (Walch XXII:2236)

Luther, however, has predicted it expressly, that one would have the same experience after his death, that namely in civil peace as well as Christian doctrine a great, sad change would occur. With regard first to civil peace, Luther once said in an admonition to penitence, " I have prayed to God with great seriousness and still ask

---

[8] Literally, "lick it up."
[9] Where a contraction appears in this English translation, it is because that German sentence contains a contraction. The translator has inserted no contraction where none was used in the original, but seeks to preserve not only the literal meaning but also the tone of the German.

him daily, that he would guide their (the papists') judgment and that he would not let any war come to Germany in my lifetime; and am certain that God truly hears my prayer and know that, while I live, there will be no war in Germany. If I die now, you should pray so, too!" (Walch IX:1461-1462). In his great exegesis of the first book of Moses, Luther writes, about the year 1540, further: And it is a great comfort that he (Is. 57:1-2) says that the just are taken away before unhappiness; thus we will also die in peace before then the unhappiness and misery comes upon Germany. (Walch I:2633)

Concerning on the other hand doctrine, we draw out of the many prophecies of Luther that pure doctrine will fall away after his death only the following. In his sermons on John ch. 6-7, he already calls to the papists,

> It would not be necessary that you rage so against us and tyrannize against the teaching of the Gospel; for the Gospel will stay with you briefly enough without that, especially when we who now preach the Gospel lay down our heads. After our death, it won't stay; for it is not possible that it stay. The Gospel has its run, and runs from one city into another; today it's here, tomorrow it's in another place...Believe, honor the Word, live according to the Word of God while you have it. Watch, don't miss it and don't sleep through it; for it will not remain forever, it will not last long. So now the best advice is that we should not think thus, that the Gospel, as we have it now, will remain forever. Tell me in 20 years how it is. When the present pious preachers who do right are dead, then others will come who will preach and do it the way the devil likes it. (Walch VII:2306, 2308)

Thus spoke Luther already just a year after the glorious delivery of the Augsburg Confession! Shortly before his death, however, in his last sermon given while still in Wittenberg, he spoke to his Wittenbergers, and to others, as follows:

> Until now you have heard the real, true Word; now beware of your own thoughts and cleverness. The devil will ignite the light of reason and bring you away from faith. That[10] has happened to the Anabaptists and the sacramental enthusiasts, and now there are more teachers of heresy around.... I see it before my eyes, if God will not give us true preachers and ministers, the devil will rip up our church with the divisive spirits, and will not let go nor stop until he has ended it. That, in brief, is what he has in mind.

---

[10] Walther's actual text is "faith; as has happened to the, etc.," but that is poor English sentence structure. The meaning is not affected by this editing.

Where he can't do it through the Pope and Emperor, he'll accomplish it through those who are united with us in doctrine....Therefore beg God seriously that he leave the Word to you, because it is going to go terribly." (Walch XII:1534-35)

Luther suspected precisely his colleagues in Wittenberg, because they had not wanted lately to express themselves rightly, that they were in cahoots with[11] the enemies of true doctrine. Master Stephanus Tucher, a true Lutheran, preacher in Magdeburg, writes three years after Luther's death, in the year 1549: "Doctor Martinus Luther, of holy memory, often said these words before Doctor Augustin Schurf and other credible people 'After my death, not one of these theologians will remain steadfast.'" Tucher adds, "I heard as much from Doctor Augustin Schurf not once but often. I'm therefore testifying to it also before Christ, my Lord, the Judge." (Unknown citation)[12]

---

[11] Literally "they were sticking together under a blanket with." The phrase used here is paralleling Luther's colloquialism and preserves the tone.

[12] Walther's citation is "U.a.D.S. 1538 ff.")

Second Chapter

What great concerns Luther's death first awakened among the Lutherans

When the burial of Luther in Wittenberg was supposed to take place, Augustin Schurf, who was then the Rector of the University, invited the students to it, at which time he concluded, "Duke Stilicho[13] used to say, 'When Ambrose dies (a famous teacher of the Church who died in 397), then Italy[14] will be destroyed,' and this prediction also came true. For after Ambrose's death, the Goths and Vandals immediately pillaged everywhere in Italy.[15] So let us consider that the death of this, our dear teacher, means hardships, which may God wish to mitigate."

When the great Württemberg theologian Johannes Brentius[16] received the news of Luther's death, he wrote to his friend Amsdorf:

What kind of wound the Church will get through the death of this dear man will become clear. Oh, that I had enough water in my head and that my eyes were fountains of tears, that I could weep, not the fallen but the remaining of my people! You will only say, 'Christ however is not dead. He still lives and sits at the right hand of His Father!'

It's true. In this, the chosen instrument of Christ has been taken away. The death of great people is in general not a good

---

[13] Flavius Stilicho (359-408) was a Roman general under emperors Theodosius I ("the Great") and Honorius. In Honorius' minority, he was regent of the western Empire. He defeated the Gothic invasions of Italy twice before political jealousies caused the emperor Honorius to have him put to death. Within two years of his execution, the Goths had taken and sacked Rome. Essentially the killing of Stilicho was the killing of the western Empire, which tottered on for another sixty-eight years after his death. Schurf's use of the term *Herzog*, "Duke," is not in the sense of the medieval feudal position preserved in England and Luxemburg today, but represents the Latin title *Dux*, which means "general" and is the origin of the English word Duke.

[14] Schurf says *Welschland*, which in more recent usage refers to French Switzerland. He is evidently using it in a broader sense to mean northern Italy, which in ancient times was considered part of Gaul. St. Ambrose was bishop of Milan.

[15] As noted above, the death that really led to that destruction was Stilicho's, not St. Ambrose's. The Church survived; the Empire did not.

[16] The Latin form of his name; his name in German was Brenz.

indication. What should we then hope for, now that we have lost this dear man? (Junius, *History of the Reformation*, IV:428)

Melanchthon himself, when he entered his lecture hall and brought the sad announcement to the students, concluded his address with the words:

Oh, gone is the wagon of Israel and its driver, he who in this terrible age of the world ruled the church! For the teaching of the forgiveness of sins and of faith of the Son of God was not discovered by human mental acuity, but revealed by God through this man. May then the remembrance of this man and what he taught be valued and dear, may we be humble, and consider what terrible darkness and what great changes will follow this event.

Immediately after the arrival of the news of death, the pious Elector John Frederick of Saxony directed a letter in true concern to the professors of theology at Wittenberg at that time, Melanchthon, Bugenhagen and Creuziger,[17] in which he admonished them to remain loyal and constant in Luther's teaching, to which they answered, on March 5, as follows:

We thank your Electoral Grace, that your Electoral grace has given us the order to give attention to doctrine, that you have concern for poor Christianity and this church and university. And though this work is a heavy burden, and much heavier than anyone can think, we still recognize our obligation, as Paul says to Timothy: "That good thing which was committed unto thee keep by the Holy Ghost."[18]

In that way, Dr. Martin, whom we remember, truly left behind for us a beautiful jewel, the pure understanding of Christian doctrine. We would also like to bequeath that to those who come after us. May God, to that end, grant us His grace and Holy Spirit.

---

[17] The German form; sometimes the Latin form, Cruciger, is seen in most histories of the time.

[18] 2 Tim. 1:14. The German text of Walther says, "The beautiful jewel which was commanded to (your) faithful hand, keep through the Holy Ghost." (It is not clear what Walther's source of that language is; it is in neither Luther's 1534 nor in his 1545 Bible; the Greek original means, "That good thing entrusted to [or deposited with] you;" the KJV is right on the mark.)

Third Chapter

How, Soon After Luther's death, a War Most Unfortunate for Germany's Lutherans, Namely the So-called Smalcaldic War, Broke Out

As soon as the work of the Reformation began, the Pope stirred up the Emperor to overcome the confessors of the pure Gospel with war, and thereby crush the work with bloody force. Already in the year 1522, Pope Adrian wrote to Elector Frederick of Saxony, "We announce to you also in the power of Christ, whose vicar on earth we are,[19] that such (protection of Luther) should not even go unpunished in this life. For we both still live, Pope Adrian and Emperor Charles, whom I raised, whose edict[20] you have mocked with great insult and disregard. Therefore you and your indulgently seduced Saxons, do penance, if you do not want to feel both swords, the apostolic and the imperial. (Cyprian, *Of the Origin and Growth of the Papacy*, 820 ff.)

However, as often as it had appeared already in Luther's lifetime that a religious war would break out, for which reason the Lutheran princes already in the year 1530 had formed an alliance for their protection, God had turned away the great misery of a religious war in quite wonderful ways until Luther's death. But hardly had Luther closed his eyes as dark, threatening clouds of war gathered over the Lutherans in Germany. The pope at the time, Paul III, as well as the emperor Charles, held that the time was now come to wipe out the spreading Lutheran church with a single stroke.

Just four months after Luther's death, on June 26, 1546, therefore, the pope and the emperor formed an alliance. In the document set up for that purpose was stated, "First, that his Imperial Majesty in the name of God," (namely the god of this world), "and with the help and support of His Papal Holiness, should begin next month to arm himself and equip himself with warriors and everything that pertains to war against those who have protested against the Council, and against the Smalcaldic League, also against all those who

---

[19] The Pope is using the royal "we" here.
[20] At Worms, where the emperor sentenced Luther to death.

are in this false faith and error in Germany, and do that with all force and power, with which he may bring them back into the old faith and obedience to the holy (papal) seat."

At the same time, the Pope promised in the treaty that had been set up to support the emperor with two hundred thousand Kronthalers[21] and twelve thousand Italian foot soldiers and a host of cavalry as well, to keep for himself. The pope also conceded to the emperor in the written proclamation that had been issued that he, the emperor, would receive half the income of the Spanish church properties and five hundred thousand Kronthalers, which he could use to deal with the costs of this war. (This document can be found in the Walch edition of Luther's works, Vol. 17, pages 1822-1827.)

To be sure, the emperor declared, as he armed for the war, that the intended military campaign had only the goal of punishing certain princes for disobedience, and that it had nothing to do with religion. Only the pope did not hold it necessary, trusting in his and the emperor's great might, to keep secret the bloody intentions as to the Lutherans, but issued a papal bull on July 4, 1546, in which he, among other things, wrote:

From the beginning of our papacy, it has been our concern, how we should root out the weeds of godless doctrine...Things have occurred, however, in such a way that the means that should have served to turn their spirits back to the right way, had to be made harsher...Thus it occurred, through inspiration of the Holy Ghost,[22] that our dear son in Jesus Christ, Charles, Roman Emperor, has decided to use the sword against these enemies of God. This plan, blessed of God, we wish to assist, for the protection of religion, with all our might and that of the Roman church. Therefore we call upon all believers in Christ, that they help in this campaign through their prayers to God and their offerings...wherewith the godless heresies and the schism may be taken away...Thus we grant the plenary indulgence and forgiveness of all sins to all (and every one) who do these things. (Ibid., 1827-1832)

So the war began, which because it was above all directed against the members of the Smalcaldic League, bears the name of the Smalcaldic War. The elector of Saxony, Johann Friedrich, and the landgrave of Hesse, Philipp, who were the heads of the Smalcaldic League, were declared to be under the imperial ban.

---

[21] The antecedent of our American dollar; "Dollar" is just an Anglicization of the word "Thaler", which in turn refers to the silver mines in Joachimsthal, Bohemia, which was, until the opening of silver mines in the American southwest, the Hapsburgs' chief source of silver. Joachimsthal's chief ore today is not silver, but uranium.

[22] (!) Is this not both a violation of the Second Commandment and the sin against the Holy Ghost?

To be sure, the named Lutheran princes also assembled a large army for their defense. Only God had decided to bring home the consequences of the manifold thanklessness of Lutherans for the good deeds of the Reformation. Thus they met misfortune after misfortune in this war.

Victorious, the emperor's armies moved through the Lutheran areas of Germany, until it came on April 24, 1547, to the final, decisive, unhappy battle at Mühlberg, a city on the Elbe, in which the army of the Lutherans, in consequence of treason, was beaten by the papal-imperial army, and its leader, the Lutheran Elector Johann Friedrich of Saxony, was taken prisoner.

The saddest thing was that a Lutheran prince, Duke Moritz of Saxony, a nephew of the Elector, actually stood on the side of the emperor in this war, while other Lutheran princes, like Joachim II of Brandenburg, remained neutral. Electof Johann Friedrich was now compelled to sign a treaty, according to which he abdicated the electorate for himself and his heirs, surrendered his whole land to the emperor, and promised to remain the prisoner of the Emperor for as long as the latter wished.

To be sure, he was supposed to give also the promise to accept the decisions of the papal Council of Trent, only though he willingly let everything worldly be taken from him, he would not let them take his faith away. Even the death sentence, which was declared to him on May 10 in the imperial camp in Wittenberg, did not make him waver.

Johann Friedrich's ally, the Lutheran landgrave of Hesse, experienced the same fate; he, too, went into the captivity of the emperor. However, his sons remained in possession of his land, while the sons of the elector were allowed only the districts of Weimar, Jena, Eisenach and Gotha. Duke Moritz, however, was rewarded for his treason with the electorate of Saxony, as with the land of the imprisoned elector.

As heavy as this retribution of God was which came after Luther's death at the ending Smalcaldic War upon the Lutherans in Germany, this war was only the least punishment that God delivered for their unfaithfulness. To be sure, the pope and emperor did not achieve their goal. Much more the word of the Lord was fulfilled: "Take counsel together, and it shall come to nought; speak the word, and it shall not stand; for God is with us." (Is. 8:10)[23]

After God had chastened the Lutherans through the enemies of the Gospel into His counsel of love, he threw away the chastening rod and helped the chastened back up. To be sure, the pope and emperor now used the victory achieved over the Lutherans to op-

---

[23] Walther's text says, "For here is Immanuel."

press them in every manner. Only God helped wonderfully, that finally, on September 25, 1555, the Augsburg Religious peace came to be, through which more was guaranteed to the Lutherans than they had had before the war, in that they were now assured publicly and solemnly, to the great anger of the pope, and against his helpless protests, independence from the jurisdiction of the pope and of the bishops, complete freedom of religion and of the divine service in the whole German empire.[24]

---

[24] This turn of events was caused by the same person who had caused the Lutheran defeat in the Smalcaldic War, the opportunistic Moritz of Saxony; as the emperor, on his way back to Austria, was traveling with the escort of Moritz's soldiers, they suddenly took him prisoner and demanded that he sign what became the treaty of Augsburg, guaranteeing Lutheran religious freedom. Charles evidently did not know what many other conquerors did—that the traitor who gives you a victory will more readily betray you than he did those to whom he really owed loyalty.

Fourth Chapter

The Sort of Disputes that Arose over the So-called Interim and Adiaphora in the Year 1548 in the Lutheran Church.

The final purpose of the Smalcaldic War had been, as we have seen, this: to lead the Lutherans back into the Roman church and to subject them to the pope. Although, however, the emperor had conquered the Lutherans physically with little effort, this crafty lord perceived that it would be quite futile if he were now simply to order the Lutherans to give up their faith. So he then decided to create a middle path and next to attempt a sort of union, in which both parts would give up something—naturally, mostly the Lutherans.

The emperor had a document set up by two learned papal bishops named Pflugk and Helding and a conscienceless Lutheran, Johann Agricola from Eisleben, who had already caused Luther so much heartache with his storming about the Law[25] and who was then the court preacher of Joachim, the Elector of Brandenburg. This document, to be sure, left Lutherans the marriage of priests and the Holy Supper in both kinds, but brought the reintroduction of many papal customs, demanded of them recognition of the pope as the supreme bishop, and in the most important articles of faith mixed horribly truth and error. This document was called the "Interim"—that means, the temporary, because this was namely just temporarily effective and was only supposed to be binding until a general council had finally decided all the controversies of faith that had arisen.

When, in 1548, there was once more an imperial assembly[26] at Augsburg, the emperor not only presented this document called the "Interim" before the estates, but also, on May 15, had it published immediately as an imperial law and commanded the Lutherans as well as the papists to accept it as a guideline in doctrine and consti-

---

[25] Agricola was an "Antinomian" who taught that through Christ's redemption the Law had nothing to do with believers.

[26] In German, "Reichstag." In most English literature about the Reformation, the somewhat confusing word "diet"—having nothing to do with what one eats, but from the same Latin root meaning "daily"—is used. "Imperial assembly" is both etymologically faithful to the German word and plain to the English reader.

tution, under the harshest threat of his imperial disfavor. As to the papists, the command was however not meant seriously; it was actually only produced against the Lutherans. In most Lutheran lands and cities of southern Germany, the emperor enforced the acceptance of his Interim violently in short order. Preachers and nobility who refused their acceptance were removed immediately as rebels against the emperor's majesty and some were exiled, some put in chains and put into harsh prisons, some even executed.

On the Rhine and in Swabia[27] alone, over four hundred church ministers, because they refused to accept the Interim, were thrown, with their wives and children, into misery, yes, in some cases killed. The well-known great Württemberg theologian Brenz, who simply did not accept the Interim, had to flee through half of Germany in order not to fall into the hands of the imperials, who were searching for him as a high traitor. One time he had to stay hidden under the roof of a house in Stuttgart, where he, in wonderful manner, like Elijah, fed by a raven with meat, was fed daily by a hen with one egg, that she laid next to him. Imperial cities that refused their acceptance, like the city of Costnitz, had their freedoms and rights as citizens taken away as a penalty.

To be sure, the emperor sought to move the pious deposed elector of Saxony, Johann Friedrich, whom he dragged around as a prisoner, to accept the Interim; only, neither the assurance of his freedom if he went along, nor the threat of harsher treatment, if he would not go along, in short, nothing, could move the heroic sufferer to give in to this temptation. Even more, he gave the following answer, among others, in writing:

I cannot leave Your Majesty, in all deference, not shown that I was subject to and instructed in this way by the ministers of the divine Word from my youth, and by diligent research of the prophetic and apostolic Scriptures have recognized, and testify to it with God and hold in my conscience without wavering, that the articles, as they are comprehended in the Augsburg Confession and what appends thereto,[28] are founded and confirmed in the prophets and apostles and the teachers who followed in their footsteps, against which nothing conclusive can be brought.... If I then am convinced of this in my conscience constantly, then I am obligated to God for this unspeakable grace, that I not fall away from the recognized

---

[27] An area of south central Germany, the chief cities of which are Stuttgart, Augsburg and Ulm. Most of it is today in the German state of Baden-Württemberg, though the easternmost part is in Bavaria. The area still contains a fair number of Lutherans but is predominantly Roman Catholic.

[28] Presumably the Apology of the Augsburg Confession, Luther's two Catechisms, the Smalcald Articles and Melanchthon's Treatise on the Power and Primacy of the Pope, as they now appear in the various editions of the Book of Concord; perhaps also some other documents not now having confessional status but on which Johann Friedrich was relying.

truth of His almighty will, that He revealed through His Word to the world. For thus it appears, the comforting and terrifying Word of God: "Who confesses me before men, him will I confess before my heavenly Father; but who denies me before men, him will I also deny before my heavenly Father."[29]

But if I should confess the Interim as Christian and blessed, then I would have to damn and deny the Augsburg Confession and what I have held and believed until now about the Gospel of Christ, and consent with my mouth, against that which I believed in my conscience and heart to be against the holy, divine Scriptures. Oh, God in heaven, that would be Your name used in vain and horribly insulted. I would betray you in the heavens and deceive my worldly rules here below with colored words, for which I would, however, have to pay dearly with my soul. For what is the true sin against the Holy Ghost, of which Christ speaks, that it should nevermore be forgiven in this nor in that world, that is, in eternity?...So I beg your Imperial Majesty not take this ungraciously, that I not consent to the Interim, but finally persevere in the Augsburg Confession and, all else put behind me, look only to how I may, after this poor and troubled life may be made a participant in eternal joy.   (See *Unschuldige Nachrichten* (1702), p. 364, ff.)

When upon this the dear prince was threatened with lengthening and worsening of his imprisonment and other harsh measures and he nevertheless remained with his confession, by imperial command his books were taken away from him , including a Bible printed on parchment and illustrated, and Luther's writings; on papal fast days, only fasting food was given him, and the like. He answered, however, that they could take from him his books, but they could not rip them out of his heart.

When the preachers who had been expelled from Augsburg were saying farewell to him answered the question of what had happened, "Gracious Lord, the emperor has hunted us and forbidden us the whole Roman empire," he said to them, while the tears ran over his cheeks. "If the emperor has forbidden you the empire, he has not forbidden you heaven; so God will surely find a land where you can preach." Upon this he had his (*Chatoulle*)[30] brought, and he dismissed them with the words, "In there is everything that I have on earth. I would like to make it a traveling allowance for you. Divided among your fellows of the Cross; and though I am now a poor imprisoned prince been, God will still give me something again."

By the way, the emperor was not as successful in north Germany as in south Germany. Even there where a few preachers and nobles

---

[29] See Luke 12:9. Translation is from the German in the text.
[30] French-derived word not in German dictionaries today, nor in Grimm's dictionary from the early 1800's; there is a colloquial French expression that means to close. Given the context, this appears to be Johann Friedrich's money box.

were inclined to yield out of fear of the emperor's rage, the people set themselves against it. In north Germany, the saying was soon widespread among the people, "The Interim has the rascal hinter'im," or in longer form, "Blessed is the man/Who can trust God/And consents not to the Interim/For it has the rascal hinter'im."

The imprisoned landgrave Philip of Hesse was unfortunately not as constant as his fellow-prisoner, Elector Johann Friedrich, but agreed to consent to the Interim in order to gain his freedom; but his land did not follow him, and even his sons, though he demanded it of them, rejected it. As Elector Joachim of Brandenburg assembled a convention of 300 preachers for the purpose of introducing the Interim, an old preacher named Leutinger from Alt-Landsberg came up and said in the presence of Agricola, who, as we have heard, had helped fabricate the Interim: "I love Agricola, I love my elector more, but I love my Lord Jesus Christ the most," and with these words, he threw, in holy confessional spirit, the manuscript which had been given to him to sign into the roaring flames of the fire; whereupon then the shocked elector withdrew from the introduction.

Already at the imperial assembly Margrave Hans von Küstrin had thrown away the pen given to him with the words, "Nevermore will I accept this poisonous mish-mash, nor shall I subject myself to any Council. Rather a sword than a pen; rather blood than ink!" Many Lutheran lords were happy to be able to say that, if they also wanted to accept the Interim, their subjects, preachers and listeners would not do it. Thus answered, for example, the three counts of Mansfeld, Hans Jorge, Hans Albrecht and Hans Ernst, to a letter of the emperor, in which they were commanded to the acceptance of the Interim:

> "Most gracious emperor and lord, in our domain it has been so, that the greater part of the people are miners, who do not have much to lose and are easily persuaded to run away, and also do not want to be pressed with great force, yet the well-being of the entire domain depends on them. And we know this much, that if we press this, that the preachers will all withdraw and thereby preaching and the Sacraments will not exist, and after the loss of the preachers, our bodies and lives will not be safe from the miners and a general uprising of the people would be expected. Dated Mansfeld, August 20, 1548."

To be sure, the emperor wrote to them from Brussels on October 19 of the same year that his order must be carried out; but it did not happen.

Even Melanchthon, otherwise so ready to make concessions for the sake of peace and unity, wanted nothing to do with the imperial

Interim. Yes, he was even more so, as he issued the first public writing against the Interim at the beginning of July, 1548. In it he wrote one could not accept the Interim, and added: "Although war and destruction are threatened, we should still hold God's Word higher, namely that we should not deny the recognized truth of the Gospel."

When he heard, however, that the emperor was particularly enraged at him and demanded of Elector Moritz that the latter expel him from his land, for he was "one of the most prominent noise makers who had stirred up and strengthened the past disturbances and uproar with their poisonous writings, no few of them against himself, the Emperor," Melanchthon was terrified. To be sure, he still spoke on November 10 (Luther's birthday) in a speech at an assembly of theologians: "Think, that you should be the guardians of truth, and consider what God has entrusted to you through the prophets, the apostles, and last through Dr. Luther." Deeply moved, he added, "The misfortune of the changing of doctrine would not threaten us, if that one (Luther) still lived. Now, however, that no one has his reputation, now, that no one warns, as he did, and many take error for truth, now the churches are wrecked, the doctrine which was until now delivered rightly is displaced, heathen practices are established, everywhere, fear, doubt and discord reign."

Although Melanchthon after this surely knew well, it was now the time to stand fast and not to enter into a union with the papists through the acceptance of papistic ceremonies and ambiguous doctrinal formulations, he nevertheless finally became soft and let himself ultimately be moved, in company with his colleagues at Wittenberg, to work up a document which to be sure did not deny the truth so grossly as the imperial Interim, but according to which through the acceptance of the imposed papistic ceremonies and through ambiguous presentation of the disputed doctrines, yes, through subjection to the rule of the papal bishops and even to the pope himself there would be an external peace established and a sort of union with the papists would be entered. Since this document was accepted on December 21, 1548, in an assembly of the country estates at Leipzig, it received the name of the Leipzig Interim, while the imperial Interim became known as the Augsburg Interim.

Far removed, however, from the peace which Melanchthon sought through the Leipzig Interim being instituted, now all true Lutherans came out against it all the more decisively, because it was put together to the shame of the Lutherans by Lutherans alone. As the superintendent at Annaberg, Wolfgant Pfentner heard in Leipzig that now children at baptism would have salt smeared onto them, that water and salt would once more be consecrated, and flags and candles should be carried around the church on all Sundays, and the like, he cried out, "

Where did they come from with this fool's work? Do they want to become children again?"

They could do what they wanted; but he could not consent personally to this. And if he were to allow himself to be corrupted this way, his parishioners would not accept it. For they had sent a letter after him by mounted messenger, and in it asked that he not consent to any godless article, or not come back to them. So he would rather have his head chopped off at Leipzig and suffer this with a good conscience than anger his church.

The Leipzig Interim found absolutely everywhere in northern Germany this decisive opposition. Hence, because of the rejection of this Interim as well, many preachers were deposed and chased out, and others were imprisoned and otherwise mistreated. The disunity and confusion rose to a high point. If a true preacher was deposed for not accepting the Interim and another put in his place, the people did not want to go to the sermon, to confession or to communion with the hireling.

The Wittenbergers favoring the Interim themselves issued the following unhappy picture: "The split would have become so great, that not only would no church with the next, but also within a church, there would have been simply no deacon, no schoolmaster, no sexton with his pastor, no neighbor with the other, no housemate with the other in unity with another."

Among theologians there broke out as a result of the Interim a great conflict, especially with regard to whether at the time when it is significant to confess, but the enemies of truth press either for the acceptance or abolition of certain ceremonies and other indifferent matters, in order thereby to confirm false teaching, to suppress the orthodox church and to draw it to themselves—if it is then permitted to yield to the enemies in those same indifferent things for the sake of unity and peace, so, if such indifferent things, because they of themselves make no difference, which God has neither commanded nor forbidden, are to be accepted or abolished for the sake of the enemies.

In this disputed question, there stood on one side the Wittenberg theologians, namely Melanchthon, Bugenhagen, Paul Eber, George Major, and the Leipzig superintendent Pfeffinger, who asserted that one can certainly yield in indifferent matters even to enemies, yes, for peace and the preservation of the orthodox church, should yield. Since the indifferent things had now been called by the Greek word *Adiaphora*, these theologians were called Adiaphorists and the disputes with them the "Adiaphoristic Controversies."

On the other side against them stood only one Wittenberger, namely the professor Matthias Flacius, with whom Nikolaus von Amsdorf, Johannes Wigand, Erasmus Alberus, Nikolaus Gallus, Joachim Westphal, and Caspar Aquila agreed. As to the last-named Aquila, the emperor put a price on his head; but kept hidden by the Count von Henneberg, he evaded the severe punishment intended for him.. In 1549, Aquila had written a sharply-worded book against the Leipzig Interim, which had the title, *Against the Despicable Devil, Who Has Now However Disguised Himself as an Angel of Light*.

The preacher Johann Hermann had also already in 1548 published a writing under the title, "That One in These Dangerous Events Should Change Nothing in God's Church to Please the Devil and Antichrist." Flacius, too, had to leave Wittenberg because of his resistance against the Interim, and fled to Magdeburg, because this city showed itself in this danger-filled time to be especially heroic; it accepted those who were persecuted because of the struggle against the Interim with open arms, and permitted that many splendid writings against the Interim were printed in its publishing houses, and to be sent from there throughout the world. This city received thereby the name "God's Chancellery," but was eventually banned by the emperor and finally had to, after a thirteen-month siege by Elector Moritz, surrender to his mercies.

To be sure, the controversy stopped with the Religious Peace of Augsburg in 1555, by which the Interim was buried. Not so the Adiaphoristic Controversies which had arisen by reason of the Interim, namely whether one could or should yield to the pressure of opponents of pure doctrine in indifferent matters and thus go into a sort of union. That question stood together with whether one should give up, on the emperor's order, the accusation that the pope is the Antichrist. In 1561, Flacius wrote that, "The dubious Lutherans now no longer hold the pope to be the Antichrist."

The Interim's supporters also forbade the use of the hymn, "Lord Keep Us Steadfast In Thy Word,"[31] while true Lutherans, like Simon Musaeus, would rather be deposed and driven into misery than allow themselves, for the sake of the pope, to be barred from the singing of this song.

This controversy over indifferent matters was only completely and finally resolved and laid to the side in 1577 through the For-

---

[31] See Hymn #655, "Lord, Keep Us Steadfast in Your Word," *Lutheran Service Book* (St. Louis: Concordia Publishing House, 2006). That hymn, though, has been toned down from its original wording in its second line. It now reads, "Curb those who by deceit or sword," The original German, "Und steur' des Papst und Türken Mord," means, "And stop the murders of the Pope and Turk.." It was a fighting song; the American national anthem similarly had a whole verse removed when, suddenly, the USA found itself allied in World War I with the same British who were mocked and reviled in that verse.

mula of Concord in its tenth article. Because now our time is a time of false union or mixing of religion and churches, precisely this tenth article of the Formula of Concord is a real chief article for our time, which we poor, contemned and attacked confessors of the unaltered Augsburg Confession cannot thank God enough, and can praise Him.

Fifth Chapter

How, After Luther's Death, a Controversy Broke Out in the Lutheran Church over Justification Before God and over the Necessity of Good Works.

The doctrine of justification, that is, the doctrine that man is justified and saved only by grace, only for the sake of Christ, and only through faith, without any merit of works, is the chief doctrine of all Christendom, yes, the actual core of the whole Christian religion, through which it is, above all, distinguished from every other religion in the world. This doctrine is therefore also the greatest treasure which had lain hidden under the garbage of papistic doctrines of men and which was, through the Reformation, brought back to light and brought forth to Christianity. There is therefore no doctrine of which Satan is a greater enemy than this one.

It is also so inseparably joined to all other articles of the Christian faith that where it is maintained pure, all other articles of faith are certainly also present in their purity and that where people are deviating from other articles, also this doctrine is not pure or will not remain pure. Luther however, had already predicted that this doctrine of justification in the Lutheran church would not remain pure, for he saw, how little it was regarded already in his time even by those who wanted to be the best Lutherans.

The dear Martin Chemnitz writes, "I shudder often, that Luther, I do not know how he sensed it, very often in his expositions of the Epistle to the Galatians and the first books of Moses repeats: "This doctrine (of justification) will become obscure again after our death." (Loci II, 201.)

This really happened then. The first of the Lutheran theologians who went out after Luther's death to rob our church of its precious treasure was Andreas Osiander. Since 1522 the city preacher at Nuremberg, he left this city in 1549 because of the Interim, went to Prussia, and there was made the preacher and professor in Königsberg by Duke Albrecht. This Osiander was to be sure a learned, sharp-minded and eloquent man, but also an exceedingly proud and intolerant man. Certainly he awakend already in Luther's lifetime the suspicion that he adhered to various unusual opinions; but as long as Luther lived, he kept to himself. After Luther's death, however, he declared, "Now that the lion is dead, he wanted to be done with the foxes and rabbits." Thus he brought out the doctrine, shortly after his arrival in Königsberg, that justification did not consist of an imputation of righteousness which Christ, through His life, works and death, had achieved and in a declaration of righteousness, but in that the eternal substantial righteousness of the divine nature of Christ is poured into people.

He was certainly contradicted immediately by the most significant theologians of our church and told from many sides to draw back from his severe error, but in vain; the proud spirit became only more stubborn. One misfortune was that Franz Stancarus, who became his colleague in 1551 and came out against him, fell into the opposite error, in that he asserted that Christ is our righteousness only according to His human nature.

Osiander died in 1552 and Stancarus resigned his office in the same year, only both had found adherents who continued the controversy among themselves for a long time thereafter, until the matter was finally laid to rest through the third article of the Formula of Concord.

The doctrine of justification was, however, attacked within our church after Luther's death from another direction and was corrupted. In 1552, George Major, professor at Wittenberg, whom Luther had warned shortly before his death against falling away and had urged him to fidelity, came up with the assertion, "I confess, however, that good works are necessary for salvation; and say publicly and with clear words, that no one has been saved without good works, and say further, that whoever teaches otherwise, even an angel from heaven, is cursed."

Later, Major only wanted to hold firmly that good works, though they are not necessary "to obtain salvation," are indeed necessary "to retain salvation." In this, Julius Menius, superintendent in Gotha agreed with Major, as did most of those who had, during the time of danger and persecution, accepted the Interim, in which Major's statement had been taken up to please the papists. As pious and innocent as that may sound to many, that good works are necessary for salvation, and as well as Major and Menius may have meant it—for they only meant to condemn publicly an empty statement of faith and punish those who considered themselves good, faithful Christians, even though they did not pursue sanctification, but remained lying in their sins. Only, as true as it is that good works are necessary, it was nonetheless false to say that good works are necessary "for salvation." That is against the clear word of God.

Paul writes, for example, "By grace you have been saved, through faith; not by works, lest anyone should boast." Eph. 2:8-9. As true as it is on the other side, that one certainly can lose salvation through evil works, it was also false to say that salvation is "retained" through good works. That also is against the clear word of God.

More, Peter writes to the Christians, "You who are kept by God's power through faith for salvation." 1 Peter 1:5. Therefore many theologians who were zealous for the pure Gospel came forth against Major, namely Amsdorf, Flacius and Gallus. To be sure, Major finally took his dangerous assertion back in 1562, as Melanchthon himself did not dare to defend it, but the others who had signed the Interim before wanted to be right in this, and thus the controversy lasted for years thereafter. In Saxony, where the Interim's supporters ruled and had brought the pious Elector entirely onto their side, those preachers whom the Majorists on the council accused of erroneous teaching, were even deposed and exiled from the land.

As it often happens now, that those who want to refute an error thoroughly, in their great zeal and carelessness fall into an opposite error, it happened then to the dear Amsdorf, who asserted that good works were not only not necessary to salvation but were even "harmful to salvation." One should certainly not think that it was possible that a pious man could set up such a horrifying thesis, according to which it seems necessary that a rightly-believing Christian must avoid with all diligence good works, as hindrances to salvation! To be sure, Amsdorf meant it entirely well; he just wanted to say that it is harmful to salvation to rely on good works and to put one's trust in the same.

But as true as that is, it was so dangerous, repulsive and offensive to say therefore that good works themselves could be harmful to salvation. That is also directly against God's clear word, which commands good works with great seriousness. Yes, Paul, the great herald of faith, says that in a change worthy of the Gospel, truly good works done in faith are "a sign of salvation" to Christians. Phil. 1:27,28.

Into this controversy entered also the Antinomians, that is, those who attacked the Law, even though Agricola, their head, had already had to recant publicly in Luther's lifetime. These Antinomians asserted namely that good works are not only not necessary for salvation, they are not even necessary to name, because they must only happen out of free love and gratefulness, so they were also within the freedom of people. Among these Antinomians were Pastors Poach in Erfurt and Otto in Nordhausen.

This controversy over the necessity of good works was only fundamentally resolved through the fourth article of the Formula of Concord.

Sixth Chapter

How after Luther's death a controversy arose in the Lutheran church over free will and over original sin.

As faithful a helper of Luther as Philip Melanchthon was for many years, it is however not to be denied that Melanchthon already secretly in Luther's last years, but after Luther's death ever more publicly fell away from several important doctrines of the Word of God. This cannot be lamented enough. For as he was an exceedingly learned and in his whole being an exceedingly lovable man, praised highly by Luther and with such a high reputation in all of Germany that he received the name "Teacher of Germany",[32] many theologians, especially the younger ones, took everything that he said and wrote as true without testing it.

Among those doctrines in which Melanchthon began already in Luther's time to deviate, and deviated ever more openly later, is the doctrine of the ability of the free will of man in spiritual things after the Fall and before conversion. God's Word says that man is by nature not capable even of thinking something good, not to speak of going (2 Cor. 3:4), that man is spiritually dead (Eph. 2:1), and therefore he must first be spiritually brought to life and awakened, newly created and newly born (Eph. 2:5,6,10) before he can do something good before God, and that God must effect both, the will and the carrying out, in man. (Phil. 2:13).

Melanchthon, however, came again and again to the teaching that man can bring himself to grace, and can cooperate in his conversion, and that therefore the conversion of man is not only through two causes, namely the Word of God and the Holy Ghost, but also through man's own will, which is then the third cause of conversion. Many students of Melanchthon then not only accepted this doctrine, which takes honor away from God, that He alone converts a man and saves him, but extended it further. They wanted to know nothing of the beautiful song, "*Durch Adams Fall ist ganz verderbt / Menschhlich Natur und Wesen.*" (Literally: "By Adam's

---
[32] *Praeceptor Germaniae.*

fall, human nature and being are entirely corrupted;" this hymn has been translated into English "All mankind fell in Adam's Fall/One common sin infects us all."[33]

As long as Melanchthon was only saying this erroneous doctrine here and there in hiding, only few dared to contradict him and attack him for this. But when in 1555 the Leipzig professor Pfeffinger and the Jena professor Strigel began to fight for this doctrine of Melanchthon as the only right one, the controversy over this point became general. On one side stood Melanchthon's blinded students, whom one called Philippists. On the other were all who did not want to deviate from Luther's teaching in this matter. Outwardly, first one side, then the other, triumphed with the help of the princes, after which ordinarily the defeated ones lost their offices and were chased out of the land. Thus, in the Duchy of Saxony, when Duke Johann Friedrich the Younger was still on the side of the orthodox, Strigel and Hügel were immediately arrested in Jena in 1559 when they did not want to sign a document in which Melanchthon's false teaching of free will was condemned. Later the Duke changed his mind, and now (1562) about 40 professors and pastors who wanted to stay with the pure teaching were deposed and exiled.

Since the error of the Philippists was chiefly in the doctrine that the dear God does not convert men by himself, but that man cooperates therein, they were called by the Greek word "Synergists", which would mean "Cooperators", and the controversy arising over this was therefore called the Synergistic. These disputes continued until they were finally and thoroughly resolved, to the joy of all lovers of the saving truth, in the second article of the Formula of Concord.

One of the most zealous, bravest and most learned fighters against the godless synergistic error was at that time Matthias Flacius. He was a professor at the university in Jena when the synergist Victorin Strigel was professor at the same university. When it came to a public colloquy in Weimar in 1560, Strigel declared that original sin is just an accident, that is, something coincidental. Flacius denied this, for he knew that Strigel wanted, with the word "accident", to reduce original sin to a mere little spot.

Strigel declared further, if original sin were not an accident, then it must be the substance, that is the being or the nature of fallen man. With this assertion, the sly Strigel had set a trap for the honest Flacius, and unfortunately Flacius fell into this trap, in that he asserted that original sin has indeed become the substance of

---

[33] "All Mankind Fell in Adam's Fall," Hymn #562, *Lutheran Service Book* (St. Louis: Concordia Publishing House, 2006).

mankind. This was, however, an equally false declaration, and it had consequences for Flacius.

To be sure, Flacius did not mean with it anything as bad as the words sounded; but, because the words, that original sin is the substance of mankind, apparently expressed something false, there arose over it a new vigorous dispute. Even many rightly-formed teachers, loyal to Luther's doctrine, for example Cyriacus Spangenberg and Christoph Irenaeus of Mansfeld, believed it necessary to hold on this point with Flacius, because he had been until then the most forceful defender of the pure teaching of Luther, and they did not want to come down on the side of Strigel, who soon showed of what spirit he was the child, in that he shortly thereafter went over to the Reformed.

Other true teachers, no matter how highly they had held the dear Flacius, had to, on the other hand, though it pained them to do so, come out against him on this doctrine, since he absolutely would not retract it. It was a great shame, that one who had until then been such a faithful fighter for the true doctrine gave the enemies this opening. From now on, as a result, it became a custom among the false believers to call anyone who was zealous for the pure Lutheran doctrine a Flacian. However, this so-called Flacian controversy was also brought to a happy end through the Formula of Concord, through its first article.

Seventh Chapter

How, After Luther's Death, a Controversy Arose over the Distinction of Law and Gospel and over the Third Use of the Law

It is well known that the Word of God contains two different doctrines, the Law and the Gospel. The Law is the doctrine of that which we are obligated to do, but the Gospel is the doctrine of that which God has done for us. The whole Bible is a locked-up and sealed book for anyone who does not know this distinction; but the recognition of this distinction is the key by which alone the Holy Scripture is opened up. The doctrine of how Law and Gospel are distinguished is therefore one of the most important doctrines of the whole Christian religion. As soon as this doctrine is falsified or even just obscured, that brings irreplaceable damage. Our Lutheran church had to learn that quickly and painfully after Luther's death.

Already in Luther's time, Melanchthon had often written in his writings that the Gospel was a sermon of penance and the punishment for sin. Since he however was using the word "Gospel" in a broader sense, namely that he understood by it the entire teaching of Christ, he was not criticized for that; for it is true that Christ also presented the Law, in which sense one certainly can say that the Gospel is a sermon of repentance, when one understands under the word Gospel not only the actual Gospel but the Law with it as well. Because, however, if one does not immediately add this, a misunderstanding can easily arise, Flacius criticized Melanchthon for this in 1548. He was calmed however at that time with the explanation that Melanchthon was understanding Gospel in a broader sense.

The so-called Philippists, however, did not only defend Melanchthon's mode of teaching, but taught further that also the actual Gospel, or the Gospel in a narrower sense, is a sermon of repentance and punishes sin. Paul Crell, Caspar Cruciger the younger and other Wittenberg theologians asserted this. Through this then arose another sharp dispute. For through this teaching that also the Gospel of Christ is a sermon of repentance and punishes sins, the sweet Gospel of grace is made into a Law, the merit of Christ is obscured by Law, the terrified were robbed of the comfort of the Gospel, and the papists, who want to make Christ into a new Lawgiver, are made to be right. Against this the orthodox theologians had to come forward in all seriousness, which then especially Flacius, Amsdorf, Wigand and others did faithfully. Only with the fifth article of the Formula of Concord did our church give its judgment from God's Word on this controversy and and lay the same to rest forever.

Another controversy was closely connected, however, to that over the Law and Gospel. The Antinomians, or attackers of the Law, said that the Philippists were right and declared that the Gospel alone is the true sermon of penance, that the Law belongs in the city hall, that is, it may be good for the police, but if one wishes to bring the godless to true repentance, one must not preach the Law to them, but only the Gospel. The Law, they said, does not belong in the church at all; it is not worthy of being called God's Word. It may be a curb which worldly authority has to use, but is neither a mirror for repentance nor a rule for a Christian life. Hence the Law must no longer be preached to the faithful, converted and born again.

At the head of these attackers of the Law stood the wretched Agricola who, as already remarked above, already in Luther's lifetime had come out with this horrible raving, but, thoroughly refuted by Luther, had hypocritically recanted his error. When he revived the already-resolved dispute again after Luther's death, he found in Andreas Poach, then pastor in Erfurt, and in Anton Otto, pastor of Nordhausen, comrades for his raving. Even Andreas Musculus, professor at Frankfurt on the Oder,[34] fell for a time into this error, but later let it go and even later served in the composition and final revision of the Formula of Concord. Also the honest Poach later changed his mind and signed the Formula of Concord joyfully.

The orthodox theologians opposed those who wanted to throw the Law out of the church and taught that good works are absolutely not necessary, like Agricola, or who taught that one could preach the Law to the unconverted but not to the converted, those who did approve of the first use of the Law as curb and the second as mirror, but rejected the third use as rule. The sixth article of the Formula of Concord is directed against these so-called antinomian errors.

---

[34] This is not the famous Frankfurt in western Germany but another city in the east.

Eighth Chapter

How after Luther's death secret Calvinists, called Crypto-Calvinists, sneaked into our church and in there stirred up very dangerous disputes.

When the cloister-prior Dr. Fleck from Steinlausig, in 1502, at the consecration of the newly-erected university at Wittenberg, gave the inaugural sermon, he made a remarkable utterance: "From this white mountain" (Wittenberg means White Mountain) "the whole world will receive wisdom." This prophecy has been, as we know, fulfilled splendidly. Already in 1517, the pious Dr. Fleck himself cried out loudly, when he had read Luther's 95 theses against Tetzel's indulgence scam, "Ho, ho! He will do it; the one we have waited for a long time is coming!" and and he encouraged Luther in a letter, "to proceed confidently, for he is on the right way, God and the prayers of all prisoners in the Roman Babylong be with him."

Thus the city of Wittenberg really became then a mountain of wisdom, but it unfortunately did not remain that. Where one has received from God great and rich grace before others, if one does not preserve it, but betrays it, ordinarily then also falls deep before others, by God's just judgment; so it also went with the once so favored Wittenberg.

With great concern, Luther had already in the last years of his life remarked that things were very dubious with his Wittenberg colleagues, and even with his Melanchthon. While they themselves didn't directly go out with false teaching and fight for it, they showed ever less seriousness and zeal to fight against it, and brought suspicion upon themselves with such false teachings, especially in regard to the Holy Supper. Shortly before Luther began his last trip to Eisleben, from which he never came back, he invited for this reason the most prominent Wittenberg theologians, Melanchthon, Bugenhagen, Cruciger, Paul Eber, Georg Major and a few other friends, as if in anticipation of his imminent departure from the field of battle, and gave them the following warning to take home with them: "That they wanted to remain constant with the Gospel; for he could see well that as soon as he died, the most prominent brothers would fall away."

"I am not afraid," he continued, "of the papists. Most of them are coarse, unlearned donkeys and Epicureans; but our brothers would damage the Gospel; because they 'went out from us, but they were not of us.' (1 John 2:19). These will strike harder against the Gospel than the papists." Luther did not content himself with this warning to his Wittenberg colleagues, but now wrote also with large letters over the entrance to his study: "Our professors must be examined on the Lord's Supper."

When soon thereafter the Wittenberg professor Georg Major was about to take a trip to Regensburg to a colloquy with the papists and wanted to take his leave of Luther, and therefore had read those words over the entrance to Luther's study, the following conversation took place: Major asked: Honorable father, what do these words mean?" Luther answered: "What you read and how they sound—well, that's what they mean; and when you come back home and I also, there will be an examination, which you will have to take as well as others will be required to do."

To this, Major remonstrated that he had not adhered to any false doctrine, but received the following response from Luther:

> You bring yourself under suspicion by silence and covering up. If you believe as you tell it to me, then speak the same also in the church, in the public lectures, in the sermons and in private conversations, and strengthen your brothers and help the erring back to the right way, and contradict the willful spirits. Otherwise, your confession is just a cover and is useless.
>
> Whoever holds his teaching, belief and confession for true, right and certain cannot stand in the same stall with others who promote false doctrine or are inclined to it, nor always have nice words for the devil and his dandruff. A teacher, who is silent to the errorists, and will even so be an orthodox teacher is worse than a public enthusiast, and does more damage with his hypocrisy than a heretic, and is not to be trusted. He is a wolf and a fox, a hireling and a servant of his belly, and may ignore and give up doctrine, Word, faith, Sacrament, churches and schools. He either lies secretly under one blanket with the enemy, or is a doubter and blows with the wind, and wants to see where he wants to come out, whether Christ or the devil will prevail; or is himself entirely uncertain and not worthy to be called a schoolboy, never mind a teacher, and does not want to anger anyone, nor speak Christ's word to him, nor offend the devil and the world.

To be sure, Major accepted this admonition and warning with thanks; later, he repeatedly told it to others without bitterness. We have, however, seen in the foregoing chapters that neither he, nor his other colleagues, stood fast after Luther's death.

Not only did Major himself, through his teaching that good works are necessary to salvation, create great confusion in the church, he also showed himself, just like Melanchthon, Cruciger, Bugenhagen, Paul Eber, Johann Förster and Paul Crell, in the controversies over the Interim and otherwise, to be a wavering reed. The worst damage at the Wittenberg university, however, broke out only after the death of the above-named. They had only wobbled back and forth failed to censure false doctrine, and communicated the right doctrine to the opponents only in friendly and brotherly exchanges of letters. They did not fight for the true doctrine, for the sake of peace, but, to please the enemies, expressed themselves with ambiguous words both in writing and orally. They had even advised that those who were upright and zealous for the true doctrine be silenced as men who sought controversy.

So, now, after their death, this was the consequence of their inconstancy and half-heartedness, that the younger ones, who were their students and successors, turned into much worse ways. These were the so-called **Crypto-Calvinists**, that is, secret, hidden Calvinists, who were so named because they held themselves forth as Lutherans, yes, held the highest offices in the Lutheran church and yet were in their hearts Calvinists and did all that was in their power to drive Luther's teaching and writings out of the Lutheran church and in their place smuggle in Calvin's teachings and Calvin's writings.

These Crypto-Calvinists, and really the most learned and influential among them, were in Wittenberg the younger Dr. Caspar Cruciger, a son of the old Caspar Cruciger, Dr. Christoph Petzel, Dr. Friedrich Widebram and Dr. Heinrich Möller, with whom several non-theological professors at Wittenberg held, for example the professor of moral philosophy Dr. Wolfgang Crell, the professor of worldly wisdom Esrom Rüdinger, the professor of jurisprudence, later electoral privy counsel Georg Cracow, the professor of pharmacology and electoral physician Dr. Caspar Peucer, Melanchthon's son-in-law, of whom the last two can be regarded as the actual driving force of these hidden Calvinists. True comrades of this clean[35] party outside Wittenberg were the superintendent and electoral father confessor at Pirna, Dr. Johann Stössel and the electoral court preacher in Dresden, Dr. Christian Schütz, as well as several Leipzig professors, Dr. Andreas Freyhub, Dr. Wolfgang Harder and others.

To carry out their scandalous plan of uprooting Lutheranism

---

[35] Walther is being sarcastic.

everywhere, and first of all in the electorate of Saxony, and of introducing Calvinism in its place under the cover of the Lutheran name, which they retained, they sought first of all to make the pious Elector August their tool. Because they knew, however, that this lord's heart was given to Luther's doctrine, they not only concealed their plans, but attempted to persuade him that they were the truest Lutherans and only enemies of those proud and obstinate disturbers of the peace, who needlessly stirred up squabbles and controversies in the Lutheran church. They called all serious defenders of the pure Luther doctrine names: Flacians, squabblers, noisemakers, yellers, Zealots, and the like.

While they rejected the doctrine in their hearts that in the Holy Supper Christ's true Body and true Blood are truly and substantially present, and received in, with and under bread and wine, and received in the mouth of all communicants, worthy and unworthy, they presented themselves as if they also believed this doctrine in their hearts, and that they were only against the tangible presence of Christ and against the gross, Capernaitic enjoyment. While they were also fallen from the teaching that in Christ the human and divine natures are united in one person and that therefore the divine nature has communicated to the human its divine attributes—omnipotence, omnipresence and majesty, they presented themselves as if they did not deny this and that they were fighting only against the madness that Christ's Body is tangibly extended throughout the world.

Those who confessed the old Luther teaching of Christ's person and of the communication of divine attributes to His human nature, they called "Ubiquitists", and informed the elector that the true Lutheran techers taught such an omnipresence of the human nature of Christ that it was spread out like a cloth, through which the truth of the human nature was completely suspended and turned into the divine, such that the true Ascension of Christ would be overthrown. They said that they were true Philippists, that is, Melanchthonian Lutherans; as Melanchthon was Luther's true assistant and only made a special effort at moderation, taught the doctrine of Luther without any exaggeration and put it in a nice, scientific form, therefore they were just enemies of all exaggerated expressions and friends of a true Lutheran, but simple and clear, form of teaching.

They took the first decisive step toward the reaching of their hidden goal even shortly before Melanchthon's death. Namely, in order to drive out the unaltered Augsburg Confession, Luther's Smalcald Articles and both of Luther's Catechisms from the Lutheran church in a mannerly way, they formed a large collection of Melanchthon's writings, in which were all of his errors and only the altered Augsburg Confession and the altered Apology. They persuaded Melanchthon to write a short foreword to this collection, and now they, without Melanchthon's advance knowledge, gave this collection the lofty title, "Corpus Doctrinae, that is, a complete summary of the right, true Christian doctrine...to a witness of lasting, united confession of the pure and true religion, whereby may the Augsburg Confession remain in all its parts to the churches and schools of these electoral Saxon and Meissen lands from now to the thirtieth year; against all lying spirits, baseless, false publication and burdens. Leipzig, 1560."

The chief hand in putting this collection together was the electoral physician Dr. Caspar Peucer, Melanchthon's son-in-law. They gave the book this magnificent title because they intended to have it introduced as the only valid collection of all confessional writings in the Lutheran church. All teachers in churches and schools, and all the other officials in the land, would be sworn to it as the norm of doctrine, to which everyone would have to conform teaching and writing.

To be sure, the book found the most determined resistance among true Lutherans immediately. The true Lutherans in Reussen and Schönburg rejected it in their solemn confession. In electoral Saxony, however, the Crypto-Calvinists knew how to push through the acceptance of their book, for they had led the elector August to believe that this "Corpus" was the best means to unite all faithful Lutherans and establish true peace.

Thus this rump book of concord was really introduced in electoral Saxony and the signing of the same by all church and school ministers was demanded, and actually with sworn obligation to teach according to it. Anyone who refused to sign was deposed, others were also imprisoned or exiled. Among those deposed were Master Johann Tettelbach, superintendent in Chemnitz, Georg Herbst (Autumnus), deacon of the same, later general superintendent in Eisleben, Master Graff, superintendent in Sangerhausen, Master Bartholomaeus Schade, pastor in Freiberg, who also had to leave the city immediately; so it also went for his colleague Johann Heine, early preacher in the same city; deposed and simultaneously imprisoned was Master Johann Schütze, pastor in Freiberg (who was however elected in 1577 to be chancellor of the university at Wittenberg).

Those who, in their refusal, called upon Luther's writings received as an answer: Luther's writings must be understood and interpreted according to Melanchthon's *Corpus Doctrinae*. By the way, the book was also introduced with force in other churches where either the prince or the main theologians were inclined to Melanchthon or entirely Calvinistic.

How the Crypto-Calvinists, among other things, wanted the Holy Supper to be taught, they betrayed already in 1561, in which year they had a truly Calvinistic rhyme printed for the children to learn by heart. One of these rhymes was as follows:[36]

> Only faith in Jesus Christ
> Causes Him to be present
> And feeds us with His Flesh and Blood
> And unites us with Him.
> The mouth receives natural bread
> The soul, however, eats God Himself.

This Calvinistic rhyme was opposed, however, in Dresden by a court preacher who remained faithful with the following Lutheran rhyme:

> The Word of our Lord Jesus Christ
> Causes that His Body is present.
> Faith alone receives it worthily
> Unworthily, he who can't believe it.
> The mouth receives with the bread
> The true Body; so it pleases God.

It was also in 1565 when the Calvinists in Heidelberg popped up with this fable, that Luther had, shortly before his death in a private conversation with Melanchthon, confessed that he had done too much in his dispute with the Sacramentarians;[37] but so that his whole doctrine would not then be suspicious, he did not want to retract what he had taught from the Holy Supper. The younger theologians would like to help in the matter after his death. Dr. Joachim Mörlin refuted this gross so-called "Heidelberg Land-Lie"; the Calvinists however were silent to that.

When in 1565 two students at Wittenberg, Conrad Schlüsselburg and Albert Schirmer, complained to their peers about the falsifications of doctrine by their professors, the latter found out about it. Peucer had them cited in December of the same year and shouted at them crudely. Yes, when Schlüsselburg persisted that his teachers denied, among other things, the true communication of the divine attributes of Christ to His human nature, Peucer yelled at him with the words, "I sh— you in the true communication."

After a few weeks, in January of the following year, the rector of the university demanded that the two students come one more time before the whole college of professors, and as Schlüsselburg stuck to

---

[36] The English that follows does not rhyme as the German does; but the translator believes that an accurate rendering of its meaning is more important.

[37] Sacramentarians: the Calvinists.

his accusation, Dr. Peucer called out to him, furiously, "You slander me as a rascal, that I am a Sacrament fanatic," and Dr. Petzel added, "You careless betrayer, you lie that I said the right hand of God was a finite space." Finally Dr. Major asked both if they wanted to retract their accusations, and as the two, for the sake of the truth and their consciences, they were first thrown into the jail, and then were declared banished, expelled from the university and chased out of the city with curses.

Since now ever more true Lutherans, since the year 1567, especially the theologians in ducal Saxony, accused the Wittenberg Crypto-Calvinists in many writings of false doctrine, Elector August, who placed full trust in his theologians, sought to set up a colloquy between his theologians and those of ducal Saxony (namely those of Jena and Weimar), to lead to an understanding. This discussion of religion, the so-called Altenburger Colloquy, then took place. It lasted, because the tricky Crypto-Calvinists only wanted to discuss in writing, from October, 1568, to March, 1569.

Instead of the peace that was supposed to come through this, the ducal Saxon theologians of the time (Wigand, Cölestinus, Kirchner, Rosinus and others) declared publicly that the electorals had been incontrovertibly exposed as false teachers in the colloquy. The elector heard this with great indignation; for his theologians brought this back to him as proof that the ducal Saxon theologians were nothing other than Flacian hate-mongers.[38]

Therefore the elector then let himself be talked by the church and school ministers of his land into demanding, besides the signing of the *Corpus Doctrinae*, from now on to sign the following declaration:

> I am not an adherent of the dangerous Flacian error, trouble-making smears, poisonous attacks and fanaticism, by which the schools and churches of this land are accused of the supposed adiaphorism, synergism and Majorism and other false publications, am not sympathetic to it, and wish, from now on with God's help, to keep myself completely away from it, damn it, flee it, avoid it, and shield myself from it as much as I can.

After the Crypto-Calvinists had even succeeded in this, they thought that they were now in such a firm position that they, without danger of being discovered, could from now on go around more freely with what they had in their hearts. If they had until now only expressed their errors orally in their lectures and among themselves, now they did it in writing. Thus they issued in 1570 a number of "propositions on the principal disputes of this time," in which

---

[38] Literally, "hate cats".

they rejected the doctrine of the real communication. In 1571 followed a new "Catechism" prepared by Dr. Petzel in the name of the whole theological faculty, in which they now came out freely with the doctrine that Christ is enclosed in heaven and that the sacraments are mere outward signs.

They declared the same errors even more grossly in two books that appeared in the same year, with the titles, "Christian Questions" and "Fundamentals". They even let the writing of a Jesuit against Jacob Andreae's teaching of the majesty of the person of Jesus Christ and another writing of the arch-Calvinist Beza be printed in Wittenberg, but on the title page of Beza's book they had "Geneva" rather than "Wittenberg" printed, in order that they not betray themselves. Hans Luft, the Wittenberg publisher, later declared that he had no longer known in this time what he should do with those books that he had previously published and were still on hand; that on the other hand, when he had printed twenty or thirty more Calvinist books were all gone quickly.

The traitors in the middle of the fortress of the Lutheran church became ever more secure and brazen. It looked according to reason as if God were with them, for everything shaped itself more and more to their favor. On March 3, 1573, the duke of Saxony, Johann Wilhelm, who had during his brief rule made his little land into a place of refuge for the true Lutheran teachers and had staffed his university at Jena with zealous defenders of the pure doctrine. Since now Elector August was now, after the blessed death of the duke, the guardian of the ducal princes, the Wittenberg Crypto-Calvinists urged the elector to depose all "Flacians", as they called the true Lutherans, immediately from their offices, to chase them out of the land and appoint peace-loving men, by which they meant Crypto-Calvinists, in their place.

It was at that time that the Jena professors Wigand, Heshusius and Melissander, the superintendent Rosinus and the court preacher Bernhard in Weimar were driven out of their office and the land after a short proceeding, because they did not want to damn the pure teaching of Luther, accept the *Corpus Doctrinae* or refrain from rejecting false doctrine. In this situation, for this cause, not less than one hundred eleven university theologians, superintendents and preachers were driven out of the electoral Saxon lands and into misery.

The Crypto-Calvinists now believed that they could dare anything. In 1574, then, they published a writing which bore the title "Exegesis," which means "Explanation." This was supposed to be an explanation of the controversy over the Holy Supper. In it was said, for example:

All purified churches should be united and pious unity should not be disturbed over this disunity (over the Holy Supper). Let us be one in Christ and drop the dangerous talk of Ubiquity (omnipresence), of the receiving of the true Body by the godless, and other similar things. Teachers should unite on a certain formula that could cause no offense.

One should make use of the modes of speaking that have been passed on to us in Melanchthon's writings. It is best to strike down the public disputations and, when those who seek controversy seek to stir up controversy and unrest among the people, it is the right thing, as Philippus[39] advised, to depose such people on both sides and replace them with more modest people. Teachers must serve unity, and speak well the churches and teachers of the opposing party.

Those were the own words of the "Exegesis", with which it recommended nothing other than a union founded on complete religious indifference, just with the retention of the Lutheran name. As insolently as the writers said this, they had not considered it less necessary to observe care that they publish the book without stating the place of publication and the year, on paper with the Geneva logo and with French type and give it entirely the appearance of a book produced in France. No one should have any idea that the book was published in Leipzig.

With that, however, they finally struck the bottom of the barrel, as the deception soon came to light. A cry of outrage went through the whole evangelical Lutheran church after the appearance of this book. Anyone who still wanted to be a Lutheran was incensed that a university that wanted to be Lutheran could issue such a book, and in such a villainous manner. So to speak, this book called all Lutherans, even the otherwise most lethargic, to arms.

Not only did Lutheran theologians everywhere in Germany write long and short writings in opposition to this "Exegesis", and some of them sent them to the elector, to open his eyes; the elector received from other rulers ever more urgent warnings about his Crypto-Calvinist theologians, jurists and doctors, namely from the King of Denmark, Prince Georg Ernst of Henneberg, and Duke Ludwig of Württemberg.

Actually, the elector had already, since his Wittenberg theologians had brought their Crypto-Calvinist writings into the light, smelled a rat and lost his previous full trust in them, and already introduced various measures to get to the truth. Until the publication of the "Exegesis", he had allowed himself to be calmed down

---

[39] Melanchthon.

repeatedly. The miserable hypocrites had therefore even still had, in 1572, the shamelessness to have the arch-Calvinist Beza dedicate and send to the elector of Saxony his horrible writing against Selnecker. But the elector wrote immediately to this aggressive Calvinist that "he may immediately spare (the elector) such writings, he would never permit that any doctrine other than that of the Augsburg Confession be shoved into his land.

Yet the Crypto-Calvinists turned everything to their favor that could be so turned, and when they had the misfortune that no plausible explanation was possible, they helped themselves with the universal means of all rascals—with deception and lies. For instance, after Peucer had denied to the elector that he had ever had anything to do with the Crypto-Calvinist catechism (see above), the elector found in a school entrance a letter of Peucer in his own hand to the rector of that school in which he recommended expressly that that catechism be introduced and declared that he had arranged for the publication of the same. But when the elector confronted Peucer with his letter, the latter actually denied his own handwriting! Similarly they denied having any part in the publication of the "Exegesis."

First the publisher Vögelin in Leipzig, who had printed the writing, claimed that he had composed it, in order to help the Wittenbergers out of their need. After he was shown that he could not have written this writing, it was claimed that the physician Curaeus, who had already left the land, so one could without danger dump the burden onto him. Yet the hour had arrived, when the net of treachery that the Crypto-Calvinists had spun around the pious elector should be ripped up.

Shortly after the "Exegesis" came out, Peucer wrote to his trusted friend, the Crypto-Calvinist court preacher Christian Schütze in Dresden, a letter, which he, however, in order to turn away all suspicion, had addressed on the envelope to the wife of the court preacher. By accident, or much more through God's gracious providence, the letter was taken to the wife of the other court preacher, named Lysthen.

She, however, without looking at the address, opened the letter and, since she saw that it was written in Latin, gave it to her husband, who handed it to the elector. With astonishment, the elector saw that Peucer, in it, asked the court preacher to give the Elector's wife Anna an enclosed Calvinistic prayer book, to put it into her hands in a good manner, with the remark, "If we just have Mother Anna on our side, there will be no problem; then we will win the lord (the elector) over, too." Now the conspiracy was discovered.

Now it was clear to the elector that he had been shamefully betrayed. He therefore now had the houses of Schütze, his father confessor Stössel and his privy counselor Cracow searched any discovered correspondence confiscated. With fury, the elector now saw that these men, in whom he had placed so much trust, had abused his confidence in the most underhanded way for their evil purposes, had played an entirely scandalous game, and made him, against his will, into a persecutor of the witnesses of the truth and of many hundred innocent servants of Christ, whom he had, with their wives and children, chased into misery.

In their letters, they had revealed their plan to make Saxony Calvinist in clear words. The Wittenbergers had all been able to receive from the three men all state secrets necessary for their safety. Stössel had even reported what he heard from the elector in confession to Wittenberg. In their letters, they had made fun of the elector's piety and zeal for the pure doctrine with biting mockery. Because the elector had arrested and then released a physician who had then betrayed secrets of the court, how they could trick the elector into introducing Calvinism against his will, Stössel called the elector in his letters a tyrant.

In the electoral court, they wrote, there was a government of women, because the elector's wife, a Danish princess, resisted them as much as she could. They also boasted in their letters to each other, how cleverly they had begun to bring their cause to the people. They had given the basis on which Luther's doctrine of the Holy Supper could be opposed most forcefully. When they spoke against the Sacramentarians, they meant people like Brenz, etc..

The next thing that the elector now did was the question to the hypocrites, whether they were Calvinists. The good elector, as he declared, planned, if they would confess that honestly, only to discharge them from their offices in the church as adherents to a foreign religion. Their answer, though, as they saw themselves driven into a corner, was the following: "That they did not want to see God's face in eternity if they had gone over to the Sacramentarians in a few matters or only in the slightest deviated from Dr. Luther's teaching."

On this perjured declaration, he had them imprisoned immediately. Even many honest Calvinists were ashamed of these Crypto-Calvinists, and declared that the fate that was finally coming to them was deserved. A few of them, like Stössel and Cracow, eventually died in despair. It would take too long to describe the further course of the proceedings against them. It should just be remarked that also the controversies stirred up by the Crypto-Calvinists, namely over the Holy Supper and the person of Christ, were finally thoroughly settled by the seventh and eighth articles of the Formula of Concord.

We do not give a historical introduction to the ninth article of the

Formula of Concord, "Of the Descent of Christ to Hell," to the eleventh, "Of the Eternal Foreknowledge and Election of God," or to the twelfth, "Of Other Factions and Sects, That Never Confessed the Augsburg Confession." Our intention was only to give historical information about the doctrinal controversies which broke out after Luther's death in our dear Lutheran church and which were settled by our church through the Formula of Concord. However, first, what concerns the doctrine of the descent of Christ into hell: there was a brief dispute in Hamburg between a few Lutherans, because the Hamburg pastor Dr. Johannes Aepinus, otherwise one of the most excellent theologians of the time, in an exposition of the 68th Psalm in 1553 asserted erroneously that Christ had to endure in hell the pains of eternal death.

Of the eleventh article's treatment of the doctrine of the election of grace, or predestination, the Formula of Concord itself says that in that regard, there has been "no division among the theologians of the Augsburg Confession" and that this doctrine is only explained in order that there "may not be disputes initiated in the future." Of the doctrines finally rejected in the twelfth article, of certain "factions and sects", the Formula of Concord itself says that these were included and rejected, not because they had become prominent in our church, only in order that such erroneous doctrines "also not be silently attributed" to us Lutherans, because in this confession, "there is no report".

Thus we cannot thank God enough that our dear church, through highly enlightened, pure teachers, has preserved so splendidly, also for the future, the unity of its true teachers and rightly formed members with the united confession of the ninth, eleventh and twelfth articles.

Ninth Chapter

How, for the resolution of the controversies that arose in the Lutheran Church after Luther's death the Formula of Concord was composed.

The time after Luther's death was a horrible time for all real Lutherans. It was the time of a thirty-year war, not so much a physical as a spiritual one, which seemed destined to end with the complete collapse of the Lutheran church. About the year 1566, a great theologian reports, it had already gone so far that the old evangelical Lutheran doctrine was only publicly in force in a few places. It was still best in northern Germany and in the little state church of Mansfeld, Reussen and Schönburg. They were already thanking God in the Reformed churches of the Palatinate that the church from which Lutheranism had come, the electoral Saxon church, had now come over to them.

The Jesuits were already jubilant that the Lutherans were no longer Lutherans, so one no longer had to preserve tolerance of their church, which had been granted to them in 1555 through the Augsburg Religious Peace. All who were not hostile to the Lutheran church did, therefore, all that they could to create peace and unity.

Writings upon writings followed in which the pure doctrine was defended and the emerging false doctrine was refuted. The theologians held public religious discussions to produce unity, such as that in Altenburg, and the princes had assemblies of princes, like that at Naumburg. The latter, the princes, instituted church visitations, renewed the obligation to the Augsburg Confession, commanded the disputants on both sides to give way somewhat, forbade the issuance of harsh polemical writings, and deposed those who did not want to keep the peace and sign the doctrinal statement that was put before them, imprisoned them, or exiled them, with wife and child, out of the land. All this was however without any success.

The division became all the greater. The worst thing was that the lapsed Lutherans claimed hypocritically that they, too, held firmly to the basic confession of the Lutheran church, namely the Augsburg Confession, interpreted however according to their meaning and understood generally thereby only the Augsburg Confession as it had been altered by Melanchthon.

Then, finally, many saw that the division that had arisen could only be helped to go away if all who still held firmly to Luther's doctrine united to produce and accept one formula of doctrine, in which the doctrine of the generally recognized earlier confessions was briefly repeated, and according to them, the doctrinal disputes that had arisen would be clearly and thoroughly decided from God's Word. The first of the theologians who took that course as Dr. Jakob Andreae, provost and professor of theology, as well as chancellor of the university at Tübingen in Württemberg, a true student of the famous Württemberg theologian Johannes Brenz.

Andreae set forth five articles in 1569: of justification, of good works, of free will, of indifferent things and of the Holy Supper. He thereupon shared them with many theologians, of whom he inquired whether these articles could not be made part of a confession through the general acceptance of which peace and unity could finally be attained. The judgment on these articles was, however, various.

Many, to be sure, declared them acceptable, but precisely the most zealous and most perceptive theologians rejected them, in part because they were not complete, in part because they contained no rejection of the opposing doctrine. Their concern was that false teachers might, for political reasons, sign, but in their own sense, and of that, evil would become only worse.

On top of that, it happened that dear Andreae, on the demand of the elector of Saxony, had a conference in that same year of 1569 with the Wittenberg Crypto-Calvinists, and in it permitted himself to be taken in and tricked by those sly spirits, so that he, after this conference, testified that they were pure teachers and that Melanchthon's *Corpus Doctrinae* contained no false doctrine. The consequence of this was that Andreae himself came under suspicion of the orthodox, that he might well hold with those hidden Calvinists or want to push for union with them.

On his journey in northern Germany, however, he made the acquaintance of the great theologian Dr. Martin Chemnitz, superintendent in Braunschweig, and only then was Andreae brought to clarity by Chemnitz on many points. This dear man, Martin Chemnitz, was also the one whom God chose as His tool to rebuild the church which was almost lying in ruins, and through whom God led this great work to be most splendid. Therefore the Papists themselves later said, "You Lutherans had two Martins (namely Martin Luther and Martin Chemnitz); if the second had not come, the first would not have remained."

When the Wittenberg Crypto-Calvinists had published those grossly Calvinistic writings, their new catechism and their so-called fundamentals, Chemnitz, who had until then worked most zealously for the preservation of the pure doctrine only in his own circle, wrote on August 9 of that year to Frankfurt to Dr. Hartmann, to Strassburg to Dr. Marbach and to Tübingen to Dr. Andreae:

> What should we do now? If we want to remain silent to this, then we are deniers and betrayers of the truth. Many pious people think, though, the best adivce is, if after an exchange of opinions, a common confession of those (false) articles in the name of all churches, to which Luther's confessions are attached, opposing those (of the Crypto-Calvinists).

Upon this, Chemnitz now composed such a confession and let it circulate among the orthodox, but waited for someone in southern Germany to raise his voice. Then that happened. In 1573, Andreae sent him "6 sermons of the divisions, which have continued from 1548 to 1573 among the theologian of the Augsburg Confession." Since however these sermons were not recognized as acceptable for a confession and were sent back to him, the indefatigable Andreae then composed a third formula of unity, which contained eleven articles, in which every time first the pure doctrine was presented and the opposing false doctrine was expressly rejected.

After this writing was presented to the Württemberg theologians and they called it good, Andreae sent it to Chemnitz and other pure theologians of northern Germany under the title, "Declaration of the Churches in Swabia and the Duchy of Württemberg." This writing, which one usually calls the "Swabian Formula", found a good reception in north Germany. However, Chemnitz and the prominent Rostock theologian Chytraeus had to correct this "Swabian Formula" in part, and revise it in part, and after this altered version was found good in Lower Saxony or north Germany, it was sent back to south Germany to be checked.

There, to be sure, this so-called "Swabian-Saxon Formula" was thoroughly approved, yet they thought it good, to let another, shorter formula be composed by the Württemberg theologians Lukas Osiander and Balthasar Bidembach, which, because it was reviewed and accepted in Maulbronn by six Württemberg, Baden and Henneberg theologians, by assignment from the prince Georg Ernst, Count of Henneberg, received the name "Formula of Maulbronn" and was sent on February 9, 1576, to the elector of Saxony.

After the elector August of Saxony's eyes were finally opened about his Crypto-Calvinist theologians, it was he who above all princes (namely, besides the elector Johann Georg of Brandenburg, the duke Julius of Braunschweig and Lüneburg, and the Duke of Mecklenburg), who now took up the work of peace and unity, so dearly wished by all true Lutherans with correspondingly greater zeal, having been deeply hurt by being until then the scandalously misused tool of the craftiest enemies of the Lutheran church that was so dear to him.

As he now had the Swabian-Saxon and Maulbronn Formulas in his hands, he called twelve theologians in whom he had good confidence to Lichtenburg near Prettin on the Elbe, and desired that they consider what the rules for the production of a proper, God-pleasing unity within the Lutheran church should be. This convention took place then from February 15-17, 1576, at the electoral palace there. The elector had invited the theologians already in a very moving letter; now he admonished them before the beginning of consultations, to give "their suggestions without regard to any person, but only to honor God and for the best of worthy Christianity."

With that, he withdrew to his rooms, where he, with his pious wife, during the important consultations of the conference, "remained on his knees and with heartfelt sighs called on God inwardly to enlighten the hearts of the theologians with His Holy Spirit and thus to lead them to the truth, to a right understanding, and to godly unity, that thereby the honor of His holy Name and the well-being of all troubled Christianity would be most truly furthered, that the matter be considered with Christian seriousness and that the controversial points be resolved." (So it is reported in the documents kept in the electoral archive at Weimar.)

The result of the consultations in Lichtenburg was a threefold suggestion: 1. That all insults given in the controversies up to then be forgiven and forgotten; 2. that no one be bound any more to the *Corpus Doctrinae* of Melanchthon, and the false books should be disposed of; and 3. that men like Chemnitz, Andreae, Chytraeus, and Marbach should be given the task of preparing an explanation of all doctrines that had arisen that were contrary to the Augsburg Confession. The Elector carried this out without delay and invited for that purpose twenty theologians to a convention at the palace Hartenfeld, near Torgau in Saxony, and not just Saxon, but also Brandenburg, Mecklenburg, Württemberg and Braunschweig theologians, above all Chemnitz and Andreae.

Chemnitz certainly had a hard time accepting this invitation, because he always worried that the Saxons, among whom for so long hypocritical teachers of error had amassed under electoral protection, would not really return with all seriousness to the old teaching of Luther. However, when they assembled on May 28, 1576, Chemnitz saw with great joy that all the assembled intended complete loyalty to the pure truth. The Swabian-Saxon and the Maulbronn formulas were forged into a third, in which much could be written more briefly, other things expanded, and German was given for all Latin expressions, so that the simple Christian would also be able to understand everything easily.

To be sure, there was no lack there of sharp disputes, but the end in everything was complete unity. Already as Andreae reported to the elector, that everyone was happy with both of the first two articles, of original sin and of free will, the dear elector answered with great joy to Andreae in a writing in his own hand as follows:

> Dear Herr Doctor!
> I thank merciful God from a true heart that His omnipotence that He has heard my lowly prayer and has been with you in the settlement of these two great points with His Holy Ghost, that the same have been brought to a good end and settlement. I will not stop with my prayer, as lowly as it is before the true God, that He continue until the whole work of this Christian assembly may be brought to the desired end. And the Holy Trinity help in that! Amen! And please you want to, as you have done, keep going; our true God will surely stand by you.

And so it happened, too. Those present hardly knew, as they were finished, how it happened to them. "The Lord did that," they all had to admit. Chemnitz, who had, besides Andreae, done the writing, wrote about this to Hesshusius, "it did not seem otherwise to him, at the end of the assembly, than if it had been a dream; the work went so splendidly above all his hopes and expectations."

After such a long time of horrible confusion and division, it seemed to them like a miracle, that God had finally given such splendid unity. The news went like a wildfire through all Germany, and everywhere it brought out such unspeakable joy, so that people thanked God publicly in the churches for it. As once in 1517 Luther's 95 theses became so quickly known in all of Christianity, that it seemed as if "the angels themselves were the couriers," so it happened again now, as Luther's formerly suppressed teaching was once more brought into the open. After the new formula, which bears the name of the "Torgau Book", was finally given to the elector on June 7, 1576, the elector had Dr. Selnecker give a sermon of thanks before the theologians departed.

To be sure the elector now received many briefs from many sides, namely from Calvinistic princes or from those princes whose theologians were secret Calvinists. In these letters, he was warned in the most urgent terms, not to allow any new confession to be made or introduced, in which the Calvinistic doctrines were condemned. Even the Calvinistic Queen Elizabeth of England[40] sent messengers to him, who had to make contrary suggestions. He and all who were assembled at Torgau certainly had no doubt that the confession established at Torgau would be approved by all real Lutherans as a pure confession in accordance with God's Word, for it had been worked out from the Swabian-Saxon and Maulbronn formulas which had been checked and approved by so many in north and south Germany.

When the theologians sent the Torgau formula over to the elector, they explained themselves in the attached writing: "We hope in the Almighty that pure teachers of the church, who bear a love for divine truth and Christian unity, do not have great reservations about this, and thus by means of God's grace a lasting, God-pleasing peace and unity can be reached and established again in our churches." The elector and the theologians just wanted in such an important matter to proceed in such a way that real Lutherans could accept the formula of unity without reservations of conscience, yes, with full joy in the faith. Therefore the "Torgau Book" was sent to all churches in the various Lutheran lands and imperial cities, with the request, that they review the same exactly and as soon as possible send their evaluations of the same to the elector of Saxony, upon which then, with consideration of these evaluations, the work of peace could be brought to a conclusion.

Now teachers in all regions of Germany assembled in churches and schools, and at conferences set up for the purpose, checked the confession that had been sent to them diligently, and sent their evaluations in. When toward the end of February of the following year (1577) 25 evaluations had come in, Chemnitz, Andreae and the Leipzig superintendent Selnecker had to, on the command of the elector of Saxony had to meet alone at the Bergen Cloister near Magdeburg, to read the evaluations that had come in together, to note all good memoranda and incorporate them, and to report on the same.

Bergen Cloister was then no longer a cloister of monks, but a Lutheran teaching institution which was maintained by the cloister's incomes. Here, in a room over the little cloister church, in which the library of the institution was located and which was still,

---

[40] Walther is not quite accurate in calling Elizabeth a Calvinist. Her own beliefs, in her words, "inclined to the Augustanan;" however, almost all her bishops were Calvinists, with the exception of bishops Guest (her personal confessor) and Cheyney, and unlike her predecessors and unlike German princes, she did not attempt to dictate theology, beyond her requirement that all preach and teach consistent with the 1559 *Book of Common Prayer*, which was a compromise of Lutheran and Calvinistic theology. It would probably be fairer to describe her as a Philippist.

until the cloister building was demolished in 1813, decorated with the pictures of Chemnitz, Andreae and Selnecker—here these three theologians, splendidly hosted by the blessed Lutheran abbot Ulner, did their work, so important the Lutheran church of all later times.

Yet even after this had happened, the elector of Saxony agreed with the elector of Brandenburg and with the duke of Mecklenburg that they should still have a few theologians take one last look through it. In consequence of that, there met in May of 1577 first once more Chemnitz, Andreae and Selnecker, further, by order of the elector of Brandenburg, both general superintendents and professors Andreas Musculus and Christoph Körner from Frankfurt on the Oder, and finally, by order of the duke of Mecklenburg, the superintendent and professor David Chytraeus from Rostock.

These six theologians then, in a nine-day session from May 19-28, 1577, read through the whole Torgau Book as well as the improvements and additions from the evaluations word for word, compared them diligently with the documents on hand, checked them conscientiously with God's Word and the earlier generally-recognized Lutheran confessions, laying and weighing every word on the golden scale of holiness, and added any improvements that seemed somehow useful. After they had now finished[41] the great holy work, and done that under God's visible gracious presence, for which they fervently prayed daily, these six men of God themselves signed this confession first, still in Bergen Cloister, on that forever memorable day of the completion of the Formula of Concord, that means, Formula of Unity, on May 29, 1577, with the following words:

That this is all our teaching, belief and confession, as we will answer on the Last Day before the Just Judge, our Lord Jesus Christ, against which we also do not, secretly or openly, wish to say or write anything, but rather intend, by the grace of God, to remain with it, we have hereby, well-conscious, in true fear and prayer to God, we have undersigned with our own hands.

---

[41]Walther: "put the last hand on"

Tenth Chapter

How the Formula of Concord was introduced into the Lutheran churches

When the precious witness of peace, by God's help despite all efforts of the enemies of a true peace, had finally been brought happily and splendidly into being, Satan now sought in any way to delay, and where possible, hinder its acceptance. The Calvinists now raised a great cry, namely that there was not, before the acceptance of the Formula of Concord, a general council, and even among the Lutherans there were a few who were for this step. Nothing, however, would have been more misdirected than to set up such a large, general synod for this purpose.

First of all, at such a council, all the Crypto-Calvinists who still called themselves Lutheran and Philippists would have appeared, and without doubt would have created such squabbling and controversy that in the end the whole assembly, wavering from the bringing of unity, would have dissolved without carrying out the task, and Satan, the enemy of all true unity, would have triumphed.

Second was that what they supposedly intended with a general council, yes, had happened incomparably more. When a few who were still discontented in 1583, at a convention at Quedlinburg, joined in the old silly Calvinist complaint that it was unjust that just six theologians had prescribed a confession for the whole church, that it would have been much more appropriate to present it to a general synod, the whole assembly remembered how untrue it was to say that the Formula of Concord was set up by only six theologians, how often the presented formulas had been sent to all Lutheran churches in Germany, how, for that purpose, synods and conferences had been held everywhere, where the formulas were checked carefully, critiques of the same had been made, the formulas had been amended and improved, and it was so that the Formula of Concord had arisen as a work on which the whole Lutheran church of Germany had worked.

The Quedlinburg convention therefore wrote in its protocol:

And there was certainly so much repeated review and checking of the Christian Book of Concord, as much as if a general synod had gathered for the purpose, to which every principality had sent two or three theologians, who in the name of all others had helped check and approve it.

For if there had been only one synod of that form for comparison of such a work, there are in this manner so many synods that were held, there are so many principalities to which it was sent and which had its theologians, with weighty and mature judgment, consider and judge it; thus, the like has never happened with any book or religious issue from the beginning of Christianity, as is clear from the history of the Church.

Thus the truly Lutheran-minded princes and city governments did not have that empty talk take place, now that the Formula of Concord was ready to go now to the work of introduction of the same into their territories. Actually they did this all the more joyfully, the more that it became clear that people everywhere did not fear it, but rather waited for it with great desire. No one was forced by threats to sign; no one was enticed into it with promises, no one suddenly surprised or shouted down. Rather, everyone was called upon to check it and speak fearlessly about any reservations one might have, and those who did this were not only instructed in a friendly and thorough way, but were given, if they desired it, additional time to consider it. There was so little thought of forcing anyone to sign that where it became clear that some believed otherwise, they were not allowed to sign. Also, no one was permitted to sign who wanted to do so with conditions or reservations; therefore no one was allowed to sign anything but his name alone. They wanted an honest signature.

Of course if it came out that a minister of church or school did not want to now anything of the doctrine of the Augsburg Confession and was a sort of Crypto-Calvinist, and absolutely refused direction, naturally he was dismissed from his service, not because he did not want to sign but as an adherent of a foreign religion. So zealously did Andreae, among others, work that the Formula of Concord be introduced and signed by the church and school ministers that he actually testified in 1578 freely and publicly: "I can truly say that no person was forced or driven to sign, as truly as the Son of God has redeemed me with His blood; otherwise I do not want to participate in the blood of Jesus Christ."

Everywhere, the state and city governments sought the most learned, blessed and peaceful theologians, who had to move from city to city to carry out the introduction and signing of the Formula of Concord. This took place most quickly. Only a few, who were remaining stiff-necked Crypto-Calvinists, refused to sign when someone called on them to do so, in the opinion that they were orthodox in their belief.

Many who had at first had reservations ultimately gave thanks for the information received and signed with joy. Absolutely everywhere, the commission was received with joy. When the commission had come to Chemnitz[42] in Saxony, when the Formula of Concord had been read to all in the superintendenture[43], the archdeacon there, Michael Sagittarius, an 86-year-old man, who had already served 65 years in the office of preaching, called out in the Latin language: "Have you finally come, you desired one, for whom we have waited in our darkness? Truth and concord were buried with Luther, and see, now I have, with the highest joy, heard that book read that leads us back to Luther!"

They had similar experiences in other churches as well. The following may serve as evidence. The elector of Brandenburg, Johann Georg, had given his commission an instruction in which the following words appear: "That they talk no one into signing, but rather admonish firmly those who have a few reservations and not let them sign until they have, in God's truth, been completely instructed and their consciences completely satisfied."

When the commission came to Berlin on July 22, 1577, they found over 200 preachers assembled in the gray cloister. After the assembly was opened with a sermon on Ps. 27:4, and with prayer, the Formula of Concord was then read, by article, word for word. As each article was read forth, the objections to it were heard and raised, and finally all present gave their consent. The chairman of the commission, Dr. Celestinus, closed with a prayer of thanks and a wish, for example, "For this rich good work, may God be eternally praise; may He preserve us and our little children in this pure teaching!" upon which, each time, the whole assembly, without being called upon to do so, called out loudly, "Amen!" Every following session was opened with the hymn, "Come Holy Ghost," and with prayer.

Yet a second thanksgiving service was also held during the sessions, with a sermon on Psalm 133, and the Holy Supper was celebrated. When everything had ended happily, they had all the bells in the city ring and went to the castle church, where the Te Deum was sung and there was a closing sermon on Psalm 110.

To be sure, not all churches that called themselves Lutheran accepted the Formula of Concord as their public confession. Part of this was because a few churches that still bore the name Lutheran

---

[42] A city in eastern Saxony; not the theologian of the same name.
[43] Equivalent to a diocese.

had already fallen away from the Lutheran faith, seduced by false teachers. Part of the refusal of acceptance was because, although the churches themselves were still properly Lutheran, yet the theologians and jurists governing those churches were either secret Calvinists or hard-core Philippists, who were dissatisfied that only Luther's and not Melanchthon's writings were recommended,[44] but Melanchthon's errors were clearly rejected, so they, with the assistance of the worldly rulers, subverted the introduction of the Formula of Concord into their churches. This was, for example, the case in Holstein, Pomerania, Palatinate-Zweibrücken, and in the cities Magdeburg, Frankfurt am Main,[45] Nuremberg, etc..

When the council at Nuremberg wanted to push through that the Formula of Concord would not be accepted, the citizens declared, "If they had no money, the would sell their clothes to get this book." Since the elector August of Saxony was the brother in law of the king of Denmark and Norway, Fredrik II, he had invited only him of the non-German princes to participation in the Concord work; but just then the most respected theologians of the Danish king were secret Calvinists, namely Christoph Knophius and Nikolaus Hemming, the latter of whom was the vice-chancellor of the university in Copenhagen. They had so deceived the pious king through lying presentations against the Formula of Concord that he would not even read it, and he forbade everyone in his whole kingdom to buy it and read it.

With these few exceptions, however, almost the entire evangelical Lutheran church of Germany accepted the dear Formula of Concord as their public confession. On June 25, 1580, at the half-century celebration of the Augsburg Confession, at which, for the first time, the Formula of Concord was solemnly published and put in print, 85 authorities of the Empire, namely three electors, 21 princes, 22 counts, 4 barons, 35 imperial cities and their church and school ministers, about 8000-9000 in number, had signed it; the number increased to 96 authorities of the Empire; for later, many more signed who had first refused to do this.

Even the Swedish church accepted the Formula at a public national assembly in 1638; in Holstein, which belonged to Denmark, it was introduced in 1647, while the other recognized Lutheran churches that did not take it up as one of their confessions have nonetheless upheld it as a pure confession of their sister churches, to the present day.

---

[44] This is not entirely accurate; the Formula of Concord does recommend the Augsburg Confession and its Apology, and its recommendation of Luther's Smalcald Articles was understood to include Melanchthon's Treatise on the Power and Primacy of the Pope.

[45] This is the famous Frankfurt.

Conclusion

Hardly had the Formula of Concord been introduced into most Lutheran churches when its imminent downfall was being predicted. The Wittenberg Crypto-Calvinist Christoph Petzel, who had fallen away to the Reformed, wrote mockingly, when a few theologians, apparently out of injured pride, withdrew their signatures, "Selnecker, too, should not worry, that everyone may rage and burst, in his words, over the Andreaean Book of Concord, which has now fallen, as a work that came not from God but from men."

But praise to God! this Petzel has proven to be a false prophet. The confession of the Formula of Concord has not only stood fast as a tree planted by God Himself despite all sotrms, but this tree has spread out its shady branches ever more widely, so that now, after three hundred years, the festival of its third century is to be celebrated here in the New World.

The hope of those who once did not sign the Formula of Concord was this: that through it, instead of unity, only more division would be created. The Holsteiner Paul von Eitzen, among others, has the main reason for his refusal to accept the Formula, only their evil hope did not come to fulfillment. As with Luther's death on the day of Concord the concord in the Lutheran church died, so it was that with the Formula of Concord it rose again from death and became the banner around which all who remained true to the teaching of the Reformation gathered in brotherly unity, and under which, in closed ranks, they conducted the wars of the Lord and have prevailed up to this hour.

Through the Formula of Concord, our church was saved from the collapse that threatened it and the understanding of the other pure confessions, the Augsburg Confession, its Apology, the Smalcald Articles and the Small and Large Catechisms, was preserved for it. When in 1577 many Reformed suggested that a common Reformed confession should be established against the Formula of Concord and openly separate itself from the Augsburg Confession, the sly composer of the Heidelberg Catechism, Ursinus, wrote to Beza, no, one should "bury the Augsburg Confession with another funeral," in that one would confess it, but secretly in a Reformed sense!

If the work of the Formula of Concord had not succeeded, there would have been no Lutheran church for a long time now. It would either have been devoured by the Calvinists or have been changed into a Melanchthonian, or Crypto-Calvinist, or United church. Having come into being in 1577 shortly before Pentecost, through God's grace it had given our church a grace-filled Pentecost.

Oh, may the day on which we undertake solemnly the commemoration of its birth which happened three hundred years ago be also a Pentecost for our American Lutheran church from which the pure doctrine of Luther is confessed joyfully to our Lutheran Christian people here, and so adorn this confession with holy life and repentance that many are won for the pure, saving truth and the Father in heaven may be praised for it!

It has often been said of the Formula of Concord that it is only a confession for the theologians, not for the untaught people. That is in no way true. Jacob Andreae already declared in a sermon from the chancel to the Lutheran people in Wittenberg, "The Book of Concord should not remain in the darkness, but be published. For it is basically nothing but Luther's Catechism."

Just read it, you dear Lutheran Christians, who do not want to remain forever children in understanding and do not want to be among those of whom the prophet says, "That drink wine in bowls, and anoint themselves with the chief ointments: but they are not grieved for the affliction of Joseph." (Amos 6:6) You will thank God for the pure and splendid confession given our church.

It is true that the Formula of Concord is not a book that pleases him who seeks only a pleasant entertainment or yet the excitement of religious feelings in the heart and looks at it only for "edification", but it contains the clear gold of pure, saving teaching, which is brought out of deep in the chest of the word of God, and the heavenly seeds, which should show the listeners the right, only, and straight way to salvation.

Oh, you dear Lutheran Christians, let us consider what it cost our fathers to craft this treasure and preserve it to the present day! What an indescribable work and effort, how many prayers, sighs and tears, how many writings, speeches, disputations and travels back and forth! What monstrous costs the pious Lutheran princes, in whose service a whole host had to work for a long course of years, had to spend on it! Elector August let the work, by conservative estimate, cost him alone 80,000 thalers, and Duke Julius of Braunschweig 40,000.

And finally, what invective, what curses, what abuse did those dear men of God who did the main work have to endure, not only from open enemies but from false brothers! When Martin Chemnitz in 1579 had to criticize the Duke of Braunschweig for a sin and hence everything came down on him, he wrote to the ducal council how his work on the Concord was proven not only "by the work itself" but, he continued, "that is testified to also by my gray hairs that I have gotten, that I should now be so paid by the court."

Oh, you dear Lutheran Christians, let us not sloppily misappropriate what our fathers worked out and fought for with such great sacrifice for us! Let us here in America take a warning example from our unhappy German fatherland. There neither the church ministers nor the people have watched seriously over the treasure of pure teaching that was given them, and thus they have, apparently forever, lost it. For while the unbelievers who have come to power there call, "Raze it, raze it, even to the foundation thereof" (Ps. 137:7), even the believers have become so blinded that they seek help by making compromises with the unbelievers here and there. They consider it impossible to restore the old, pure, unfalsified Christianity, and the consequence of that is that they—lose everything.

Already in 1524, Luther called to his German Christian people:

> Dear Germans, buy while the market is in front of your door; gather while it shines and the weather is good; use God's grace and Word, while it is here. For this you should know: God's Word and grace is a moving rainfall that does not come again to where it has once been. He was with the Jews; but gone is gone; now they have nothing. Paul brought Him to Greece; gone is also gone; now they have the Turk. Rome and the Latin land also had Him; gone is gone; now they have the Pope. And you Germans must not htink, that you will have Him forever, for the ingratitude and disregard will not let Him stay. Therefore grasp and hold, whoever can grasp and hold; lazy hands must have a bad year.

Let that be said to you, too, dear Lutheran Christian people of North America! God has also overtaken you in this time with His pure Word and unfalsified Sacrament. Oh, hear then also the voice of your God and Savior:

Hold thou fast what thou hast, that no man take thy crown. (Rev. 3:11)

Formula of Concord

Epitome

Comprehensive Summary
of the
Disputed Articles

between the theologians of the Augsburg Confession in the following repetition, explained and compared according to the guidance of God's Word

Remark: The Formula of Concord is called a "repetition" here because it is not presented as a new, altered confession of faith of the Lutherans, but rather only that the Augsburg Confession should be repeated in its genuine sense.

OF THE COMPREHENSIVE SUMMARY, RULE AND NORM

according to which all doctrine should be judged, and the errors which have appeared should be decided and explained in a Christian way.

1. We believe, teach and confess, that the only rule and norm according to which all doctrines and teachers alike should be assessed and judged is the prophetic and apostolic Scriptures of the Old and New Testaments alone, as is written, "Thy Word is a lamp unto my feet and a light unto my path." Ps. 119. And St. Paul: "[Though we, or] an angel from heaven, preach any other Gospel...let him be accursed." Gal. 1.

Other writings, however, of the old or new teachers, as they are named, should not be held equal with the holy Scripture, but rather all together be subjected [to Scripture] and not be accepted otherwise than as witnesses, in what form and at what places such doctrine of the prophets and apostles was preserved.

With this, its first and highest principle, that the Scriptures of the Apostles and Prophets are the only rule and norm of all doctrine and teachers, our church rejects all teachings of men taken from reason, or from traditions, or from supposed new revelations, in matters of faith and who present such teachings.[46]

2. And after, right after the time of the Apostles, also in their lifetime, false teachers and heretics broke in, and, against them, creeds, that is, short, concise confessions, were adopted, which were held as the general Christian faith and confession of the orthodox and true churches, namely the Apostles' Creed, Nicene Creed, and Athanasian Creed: we confess the same, and reject hereby all heresies and teachings contrary to them that have been introduced into the Church.

In that the Formula of Concord confesses the three old general Creeds, it testifies that the Lutheran church has not separated itself from the old general Christian church, is not new, but nothing other than a true daughter of the old general holy Christian Church. The three general Creeds also show that the the Christian Church already from the time of the apostles established and had creeds or church confessions of faith.

3. As far as the division in matters of faith that has occurred in our times is concerned, we hold as the unanimous consensus and declaration of our Christian faith and confession, especially against the papacy and its false church service, idolatry, superstition and other sects, our confessions: the first, unaltered Augsburg Confession that was given to emperor Charles V at Augsburg in Year 30 [1530], together with its apology, the articles that were established at Smalcald in Year 37 [1537] and signed by the most eminent theologians of that time.

It is with emphasis that the "unaltered" Augsburg Confession is named here, because there was also an altered and falsified edition of the same in 1540 by Melanchthon.

And because such things also affect the ordinary laity and their souls, we also confess the small and large Catechisms of Doctor Luther, as they appear in the *Books of Luther*, as a Bible for the

---

[46] Walther's annotations to the text are in bold face.

laity in which all is comprehended extensively that is in the Holy Scripture and is necessary for a Christian to know for his salvation.

> By the "ordinary laity" the simple Christians are meant who are still very weak in understanding.
> By the *Books of Luther* are meant Luther's works who were printed together just before and after Luther's death in Jena and Wittenberg.
> The Catechism is called the "Bible of the Laity" because in it even the simplest have a nice summary of the Bible.

All doctrines should be established according to this guidance, as given above, and what is against our unanimous declaration of our faith, should be rejected and condemned.

Such form will maintain the distinction between the Holy Scripture of the Old and New Testament and all other writings, and the Holy Scripture alone remains the only judge, rule and norm, according to which, as the only proof-stone, all doctrines should and must be recognized and judged, whether they are good or evil, right or wrong.

The other creeds and the other writings adduced, however, are not judges like the Holy Scripture, but only witness and explanation of the faith, as to how the Holy Scripture at all times was understood and explained in disputed articles in the churches of God by those then living, and contrary doctrine was rejected and condemned.

> Thus the creeds of the orthodox[47] Church are not actually judges, but only testimonies, but not testimonies of error, but of the truth, as then our fathers say expressly in the "Repetition," that they, as they make the foundation "God's Word as the eternal truth, thus also these writings (namely the Confessions) as the testimony of the truth and to introduce and take up the unanimous understanding of our predecessors who remained constantly with the pure doctrine."

---

[47] Meaning here churches that teach the right doctrine, not the churches, mostly in eastern Europe, that call themselves "Orthodox.."

I
Of Original Sin

STATUS OF THE CONTROVERSY

The Main Question in this Division

Whether original sin is actually and without any distinction of people the corrupted nature, substance and being, or actually the most prominent and best part of his being, as the reasonable soul itself in its highest grade and powers? Or whether there is a difference between a person's substance, nature, being, body and soul also after the fall, and original sin is a difference, thus that the nature is one thing and original sin is another, which is stuck in the corrupted nature and which corrupts nature?

Since the Formula of Concord had the purpose of clearing up and setting aside the doctrinal disputes that arose after Luther's death, it gives in every article first, what the point of contention was.

AFFIRMATIVE

Pure teaching, belief and confession derived from the foregoing norm and summary explanation.

1. We believe, teach and confess, that there is a distinction between human nature, not only as it was created by God in the beginning pure and holy without sin, but also as we now have it after the Fall, namely between the nature as it also after the Fall is and remains a creature of God, and the original sin, and that such a distinction is as great as the difference between God's and the devil's work.

2. We also believe, teach and confess that this distinction must be maintained with greatest diligence, because this teaching that there is supposedly no distinction between our corrupted human nature and original sin goes against the chief articles of our Christian faith of the creation, redemption, sanctification and resurrection of our body and cannot coexist with those [articles].

For not only Adam's and Eve's body before the Fall, but also our body and soul after the Fall, notwithstanding that it decays, is made by God, which God also still recognizes as His work, as is written in Job 10: "Thine hands have made me and fashioned me together round about."

The Son of God in the union of His Person took on such a human nature, though without sin, and thus not an alien body but our flesh upon Himself, and became according to the same our physical brother. Heb. 2: "Forasmuch then as the children are partakers of flesh and blood, he also himself likewise took part of the same." Also: "For verliy he took not on him the nature of angels; but he took on him the seed of Abraham. Wherefore in all things it behoved him to be made like unto his brethren," excepting sin. Thus Christ has redeemed it as His work, sanctifies it as His work, awakes it from the dead and adorns it splendidly as His work. But He did not create original sin, nor accepted it, nor redeemed it, nor sanctified it, and will not raise it to the Elect, nor adorn or save it, but rather, in the resurrection, will utterly destroy it.

From that, the distinction between the corrupted nature and the corruption that sticks in nature whereby nature has been corrupted, is easily to be recognized.

3. We believe, teach and confess, however, on the other hand, that original sin is not a slight, but such a deep, corruption of human nature that nothing healthy or uncorrupted in the body and soul of a person, to his inward or outward powers, has remained, but as the Church sings, "Through Adam's fall, human nature and being are completely corrupted."[48]

What unspeakable damage can be recognized, not by reason but only by God'sWord, and that no one can separate nature and such corruption of nature, but God alone, which has completely happened, for our nature, that we now bear, without original sin and separated and taken away from it, will arise and live eternally, as is written in Job 19: "I shall be enclosed in this my skin, and will, in my own body, see God; I will see Him, and my eyes will look upon Him."[49]

NEGATIVE

Rejection of the false opposing doctrine.

1. According to the same, we reject and condemn when it is taught that original sin is only a *reatus* or debt created by another, without being any corruption of our nature.

This is an error of the papists.

2. Likewise, that evil lusts are not sin, but created, essential characteristics of nature, as if this defect or damage is not really

---

[48] See "All Mankind Fell in Adam's Fall," Hymn #369, *The Lutheran Hymnal* (St. Louis: Concordia Publishing House, 1941).
[49] Luther's 1534 Bible.

sin for which a person outside of Christ should be a child of wrath.

This is an error of the Pelagian sect that arose in the fifth century, but which the papists later accepted.

3. For the same reason we also reject the Pelagian error, which claims that human nature remained uncorrupted and, especially in spiritual things, completely good and pure in its natural forces.

4. Also, that original sin is only a slight, unimportant spot or a flaw that flew into it, under which nature retained its good powers also in spiritual things.

This is an erroneous teaching of the Scholastics, respected papal theologians in the 11th to 16th centuries, and of a few papists also in later times.

5. Also, that original sin is only a superficial hindrance to the good spiritual powers, and not a robbing or lack of the same, like when a magnet is smeared with garlic juice, through which its natural power is not taken away, but only hindered; or that the same fault can be wiped away easily like a spot from the face or paint from a wall.

This is the erroneous teaching of the Semi-Pelagians who emerged in France in the fifth century, the Scholastics, and the false Lutherans who were called Synergists.

6. Also, that in a person, human nature is not entirely corrupted, but the person still has something good in him, also in spiritual things, such as capacity, skill, diligence or in spiritual things the ability to start, do, or cooperate in doing something.

This, too, was an erroneous teaching of the Synergists.

7. Against that we also reject the false doctrine of the Manichaeans, when it is taught that original sin is something substantial and independent poured into nature and mixed with it by Satan, as poison and wine are mixed.

8. Also, that not the natural person, but something other and alien in a person sins, therefore not nature, but only the original sin in the nature is accused.

The Manichaeans were a horrible sect that arose in Persia, more heathen than Christian, to which Augustine adhered before his conversion.

9. We reject and condemn also as a Manichaean error when it is taught that original sin is actually and without any distinction the substance, nature and being of the corrupted person, thus that no difference between the corrupted nature after the fall itself and original sin can be thought, nor that one can in one's thoughts distinguish them.

This is the error of the adherents of Flacius, the so-called Flacians, who not only asserted—rightly—that orig-

inal sin cannot be separated from human nature in this life, but that they cannot be distinguished.

10. Such original sin is, however, called "nature sin, personal sin, sin in being," by Luther, not that the nature, person or being of a person is itself, without distinction, original sin, but that with such words, the distinction between original sin, as it is in human nature, and the other sins, that one calls real sins, can be shown.

The expressions of Luther, "nature sin" and "personal sin" are mentioned here because the Flacians wanted to justify their error and make it look better.

11. For original sin is not a sin that one does, but it sticks in the nature, substance and being of a person, so, even when no wicked thought arises in the heart of the corrupted person any more, no useless word is spoken, nor bad deed happen: even so, the nature is corrupted through original sin, which is born into us in the sinful seed and is the source of all other real sins, like bad deeds, words and thoughts, as is written: "Out of the heart come evil thoughts."[50] Again, "The imagination of man's heart is evil from his youth."[51]

12. It is well to note the differing understanding of the word "nature", through which the Manichaeans cover their error and cause many simpler people to err. For at times it means the human being, as when it is said, "God made human nature." At other times, however, it means the kind of thing that is in the nature or being, as when it is said, "It is the nature of snakes to bite, and human nature and way is to sin," since the word "nature" does not mean the substance of a person, but means something that is in the nature or substance.

False teachers like to try to slip in secretly; they therefore like to use such words as have various meanings, to trick their listeners. The way of pure teachers, however, is to speak and to write as clearly as possible.

13. Concerning the Latin words *substantia* and *accidens*, however, because those are not words of the Holy Scripture, and are also unknown to the common man, they should not be used in sermons in front of the ordinary, uncomprehending people, but should be spared the simple people.

But in school among the learned, because they are well-known and can be used without any misunderstanding, through which the essence of a thing, and what pertains to it incidentally, can actually be distinguished, such words are retained properly in the disputation about original sin.

For the difference between God's and the devil's work is most

---

[50] No citation by Walther; the quotation is from Matt. 15:19.
[51] Gen. 8:21.

clearly shown through it, because the devil can create no substance, but only, in an incidental way, from God's decree, corrupt the substance God has created.

The Flacians asserted that it is false to say that original sin is just an *accidens*, that is, just something incidentally pertaining to the nature of people; that one must rather teach that original sin is the *substantia*, that is, the essence of the person himself.

II
Of Free Will

STATUS OF THE CONTROVERSY

The chief question in this division.

Since the human will is found in four unequal conditions, namely: 1. before the Fall; 2. after the Fall; 3. after rebirth; 4. after the resurrection of the body, the main question is solely of the will and capacity of a person in the second state, what kind of powers he has on his own after the fall of our first parents and before his rebirth in spiritual things, and whether he is able of his own powers, before and until he is reborn through the Spirit of God, to fit and prepare himself for the grace of God, and to receive the grace offered in the Word and Holy Sacraments, or not?

AFFIRMATIVE

True Doctrine, according to God's Word, of this article.
1.   Of this it is our teaching, belief and confession that the understanding and reason of a person in spiritual things is that he is blind and understands nothing by his own powers, as is written: "The natural man receiveth not the things of the Spirit of God; for they are foolishness unto him; neither can he know them, because they are spiritually discerned"[52] when he is asked about spiritual things.

Thus a person has by nature no freedom in his intentions from his own understanding.
2.   Likewise we believe, teach and confess that a person's unregenerate will is not only turned away from God but has become

[52] 1 Cor. 2:14

an enemy of God, that he has only desire and will for evil and what is against God, as is written: "The imagination of man's heart is evil from his youth." Again: "To be fleshly-minded is an enmity against God, since it is not subject to the Law, for it is not capable of that." Yes, as little as a dead body can make itself alive again to a physical, earthly life, just as little can a person, who is spiritually dead through sin, raise himself to spiritual life, as is written: "Even when we were dead in sins, hath quickened us together with Christ." (Eph. 2:5) Therefore we are not "sufficient of ourselves to think any thing as of ourselves, but our sufficiency is of God." (2 Cor. 3:5).

Thus a person has by nature in the spiritual no freedom also in his intentions 2. from his own will.

3. God the Holy Ghost, however, does not work conversion without means, but uses the preaching and hearing of God's Word, as is written: "The Gospel is the power of God unto salvation." It is God's will that one should hear His Word and not block one's ears. In that Word, the Holy Ghost is present and puts into hearts that they, like Lydia in Acts 16, pay attention and thus become converted solely through the grace and power of the Holy Ghost, Whose work alone the conversion of people is. For without His grace, our willing and running, our planting, sowing and watering are all nothing, if He does not also grant the flourishing, as Christ says, "Without me you can do nothing." With what short words, he denies the free will its powers and ascribes everything to the grace of God, in order that no one can boast before God. 1 Cor. 1.

NEGATIVE

Contrary false teaching.

Accordingly, we reject and condemn all the following errors as contrary to the norm of God's Word:

1. The raving of the philophers who were called Stoics, and also the Manichaeans, who taught that everything that happens must happen so and cannot happen otherwise, and that one does everything by compulsion, including in outward things, and is compelled to evil works and deeds such as unchastity, robbery, murder, theft and the like.

The Stoics were a heathen sect founded in the fourth century BC by Zeno; the Manichaeans have been described previously.

2. We also reject the error of the gross Pelagians, who taught that a person can by his own powers, without the grace of the Holy Ghost, can convert himself to God, believe the Gospel, obey the Law of God from his heart, and thus can earn forgiveness of sins and

eternal life.

3. We also reject the error of the Semi-Pelagians, who teach that a person can by his own powers begin his conversion, but without the grace of the Holy Ghost cannot complete it.

4. Also, where it is taught that although a person with his free will before his regeneration is too weak to begin converting himself to God by his own powers and to be obedient to God's Law in his heart, however, when the Holy Ghost has made a beginning with preaching and has offered His grace, that then the will of a person and his own natural powers to some degree can do something, however little and weakly, and help and cooperate to fit and prepare himself for grace, and grasp, accept and believe the Gospel.

> **This was an error of the false Lutherans, who are called Synergists.**

5. Also, that a person, after he is converted, can obey and completely fulfill the Law of God, and that such fulfillment is our righteousness before God, with which we earn eternal life.

> **This was an error of the papalists. That a person already in this life can become completely holy is taught now notably by the Methodists.**

6. Also, we reject and condemn the error of the Enthusiasts* who teach that God justifies and saves people without means and draws them to Himself, without the hearing of the Word of God, also without the use of the holy Sacraments.

> **The old Enthusiasts were a sect that arose in the fourth century, also called Euchites or Messalians; newer Enthusiasts were the Anabaptists and Schwenkfelders in the sixteenth century.**[53]

7. Also, that God, in conversion and regeneration, completely destroys the substance and being, and especially the reasonable soul, and creates in conversion and regeneration a new being of the soul out of nothing.

> **This was an error of the Flacians.**

8. Also, when these sayings are used without explanation, that the human will works against the Holy Ghost before, in and after conversion, and that the Holy Ghost is given to those who strive against him intentionally and persistently because God "makes willing out of the unwilling, and lives in the willing," as Augustine says.

> **Flacius used such expressions, in which he referred to the**

---

* "Enthusiasts" means those who expect the heavenly enlightenment of the spirit without the preaching of the Word of God. (Walther's comment).

[53] The most obvious form of Enthusiasm in the 21st century Church would be the Pentecostal and Charismatic movements in the churches.

conversion of Paul, which was, however, extraordinary.

Concerning then the sayings of the old and new church teachers, as it is said: "God draws, but draws those who want it," or again, "The will of a person is not idle in conversion, but does something." Because such sayings are used to confirm the natural free will of a person in conversion against the doctrine of the grace of God, we hold that they are not similar to the form of healthy doctrine, and accordingly, when speaking of conversion to God, it is better to avoid them.

The saying: "God draws, but draws those who want it," was used by Chrysostom among the old teachers; The saying, however: "The will of a person is not idle in conversion," etc., was used by the Scholastics, and among the newer teachers by Melanchthon and above all the Synergists.

Against that it is properly said that God draws and makes willing people out of unwilling, oppositional people, and that after such conversion, the regenerate will, in daily practice, is not idle but cooperates in all works that the Holy Ghost does through us.

9. Also, that Dr. Luther wrote that the will of a person in his conversion is purely passive, that is, that it does absolutely nothing, that this is to be understood as being when the Spirit of God attacks the human will and works the new birth and conversion through the heard Word or through the use of the holy Sacraments. For when the Holy Ghost has done this, and has changed the human will solely by His divine power and work, then the new will of a person is an instrument and tool of God the Holy Ghost, that it no longer only accepts grace, but also cooperates in the works of the Holy Ghost that follow.

Thus there are, before the conversion of a person, only two real causes, namely the Holy Ghost and the Word of God, as the instrument of the Holy Ghost, through which He works conversion, which a person should hear, but not by his own powers, but only through the grace and working of the Holy Ghost can give and accept faith.

Melanchthon taught erroneously that there are three effective causes of conversion: the Word of God, the Holy Ghost, and a person's own cooperating will.

III
Of Justification of Faith before God

STATUS OF THE CONTROVERSY

Main Question in this Division

Because clearly, by virtue of God's Word and according to the content of the Augsburg Confession, it is confessed that we poor sinners are only justified and saved before God through faith in Christ, and so only Christ, who is true God and man, is our righteousness, because in him the divine and human natures are personally united with each other (Jer. 23; 1 Cor. 1; 2 Cor. 5), a question has arisen: according to which nature is Christ our righteousness? and thus two opposite errors have come into some churches.

For the one part has held that Christ is our righteousness only according to his divinity, when he dwells in us through faith, against which indwelling [by faith] Godhead all people's sin is to be regarded as a drop of water against the great sea. On the other hand, others have held that Christ is our righteousness before God only according to his human nature.

AFFIRMATIVE

Pure Doctrine of the Christian Churches against both the above Errors

1. Against both the above errors, we believe, teach and confess unanimously that Christ is our righteousness neither by his divine nature alone, nor by his human nature alone, but rather the whole Christ according to both natures is alone in his obedience, which he has, as God and man, rendered to the Father until death, and earned thereby forgiveness of sins and eternal life, as it is written: "For as by one man's disobedience many were made sinners, so by the obedience of one shall many be made righteous." Rom. 5:19[54]

2. Next, we believe, teach and confess that our righteousness before God is that God forgives sin out of pure grace without any of our previous, present or following works, earning or merit, and grants and imputes to us the righteousness of the obedience of Christ, for the sake of which righteousness we are taken up into God's grace and are held to be righteous.

---

[54] Walther incorrectly cites Rom. 2.

3. We believe, teach and confess that only faith is the means and tool with which we apprehend Christ and thus, in Christ, such righteousness, for the sake of which such faith is reckoned to us as righteousness. Rom. 4.

4. We believe, teach and confess that this faith is not a bare recognition of the stories of Christ, but are such a gift of God through which we recognize Christ, our Savior, properly in the word of the Gospel and trust in him, that we solely for the sake of his obedience, by grace, have forgiveness of sins, are held by God the Father to be pious and righteous, and are eternally saved.

5. We believe, teach and confess that in the manner of the holy Scripture, the word "justify" in this article means "absolve", that is, to pronounce one free of sins. "Whoever pronounces the Godless just, and damns the righteous, is an abomination before the LORD."[55] Also, "Who wants to accuse the elect of God? It is God who makes just."

And because at the same place the words regeneration and vivification are used, as happens in the Apology, that it happens with the same understanding, through which otherwise the renewal of a person is understood and is distinguished from the justification of faith.

6. We also believe, teach and confess, notwithstanding that much weakness and sin still remain with the true believers and the truly reborn until the grave, that they should doubt neither their righteousness, as it is reckoned to them through faith, nor the salvation of their souls, but rather that they should hold it as certain that they, for Christ's sake, by the promise and Word of the holy Gospel, have a gracious God.

7. We believe, teach and confess that for the preservation of pure doctrine of the justification of faith before God through the "exclusive particles", that is, the following words of the holy apostle Paul, through which the merit of Christ is entirely separated from our works and only Christ is given the honor, are to be kept with particular diligence, for the holy apostle Paul writes, "By grace, without merit, without law, without work, not by works," which words all together mean that only through faith in Christ do we become justified and saved.[56]

8. We believe, teach and confess that although preceding contrition and following good works do not belong in the article on justification before God, nevertheless there should not be invented such a faith that can exist and remain together with an evil intent to sin and to act contrary to conscience. Rather, after a person is jus-

---

[55] Prov. 17:15.
[56] Walther omits the citations: Eph. 2:8; Rom. 1:17; 3:24; 4:3 ff.; Gal. 3:11; Heb. 11. (In Walther's time, Pauline authorship of Hebrews was widely accepted.)

tified through faith, then a true, live faith is active through love. Gal. 5. Thus, that good works always follow and are found together with a justifying faith, where it is rightly formed, as it is never alone, but always has with it love and hope.

The papists teach that one can have true faith even though he lives in mortal sin.

ANTITHESIS or NEGATIVE

CONTRARY TEACHING REJECTED

Accordingly, we reject and condemn all the following errors:

1 That Christ is our righteousness solely through the divine nature.
This was the error of Andreas Osiander.

2. That Christ is our righteousness solely through the human nature.
This was the error of Stancarus.

3. That in the sayings of the prophets and apostles, where the justification of faith is discussed, the words justify and be justified should not mean to be declared free of sin, and to attain forgiveness of sins, but rather, caused by the infusion by the Holy Ghost of love, virtue and the works that follow, to be made righteous by deeds before God.
This is the error of the papists, which also appeared in the Interim Book.

4. That faith regards not only the obedience of Christ but also His divine nature, as the same lives and works in us, and through such indwelling our sins are covered.
Error of A. Osiander.

5. That faith is such a trust in the obedience of Christ as can be and remain in a person who is at the same time not truly repentant, where also no love follows, but persists against his conscience in sin.
Error of the papists, which also appeared in the Interim Book.

6. That not God himself, but only the gifts of God dwell in the believers.
So taught a few Scholastics.

7. That faith saves because renewal in the love of God and one's neighbor begins in us through faith.
Error of the papists.

8. That faith has the first place in justification, but at the same time renewal and love belong to our righteousness before God, insofar as although they are not the chief cause of our justification, still our righteousness before God is not complete without them.
An error that appeared in the Interim Book

9. That the faithful are justified before God and are saved through both the imputed righteousness of Christ and through the new obedience that has begun, or in part through the imputation of the righteousness of Christ, in part, however, through the new obedience that has begun.

Error that appeared in the Interim Book.
10. That the promise of grace is appropriated to us through faith in the heart, and through the confession that occurs orally, and through other virtues.
Error of Georg Major in Wittenberg.

11. That faith does not justify without good works, thus, that good works, without the presence of which a person cannot be justified, are required for righteousness.
Error of the Crypto-Calvinists, that is, the secret Calvinists in the Electorate of Saxony.

IV
Of Good Works

STATUS OF THE CONTROVERSY

The chief question in the dispute over good works

There were two divisions in some churches over the doctrine of good works:
1. First, several theologians divided over the following sayings, in that some wrote: Good works are necessary to salvation; it is impossible to be saved without good works. Likewise: No one has ever been saved without good works. The others, however, wrote: Good

works are harmful to salvation.

2. After that there was also a division between several theologians because one faction argued with regard to the words "necessary" and "free", one need not use those words of new obedience, which does not flow from need and compulsion, but from a free spirit; the other faction held that use of the word was necessary, because such obedience does not stand in our caprice, but rather regenerate men are obligated to render such obedience.

From this dispute over the words there was afterward a dispute over the issue itself, that one side argued, one should absolutely not promote the Law among Christians, but only admonish the people to good works from the holy Gospel; the other side contradicted that.

AFFIRMATIVE

Pure Doctrine of the Christian Churches in This Dispute

For a thorough explanation and disposition of this division, our teaching, belief and confession is this:

1. That good works follow true faith, when the same is not dead, but a lively faith, certainly and without doubt, as fruits of a good tree.

2. We believe, teach and confess also that good works should be excluded just as much when the question is of salvation as with the article on justification before God, as the Apostle testifies with clear words, as he wrote: As David also says, that salvation belongs only to the person to whom God imputes righteousness, without contribution of works, as he says, "Blessed are those to whom their unrighteousness is not imputed." Rom. 4. And again: "By grace you have been saved; it is God's gift, not by works, that someone might boast." Eph. 2.

3. We believe, teach and confess also that all people, especially, however, those who have been born again and renewed by the Holy Ghost, are obligated to do good works.

4. In which sense the words "necessary," "should" and "must" are to be used properly and in a Christian way also of the regenerate, and are in no way contrary to the example of healthy words and sayings.

5. However, through the said words "necessity" and "necessary", when spoken of the regenerate, should not be understood a compulsion, but solely the obedience owed, which true believers, as many as are born again, render not by force or driven by the Law, but from a free spirit; because they are no longer under the Law, but under grace.

6. Accordingly, we also believe, teach and confess that when it is said, "The regenerate do good works out of a free spirit, is should not be understood as if it is within the caprice of the regenerate man to do good works or leave them alone, when he wishes, and at the same time retain faith, when he intentionally persists in sins..

7. Which should not be understood otherwise than as the Lord Christ and the Apostles explain it, namely, of the liberated spirit, that he does not do it out of fear of punishment but out of love for righteousness, like children. Rom. 8.

8. However, this voluntariness is not perfect in the elect children of God, but is burdened with great weakness, as St. Paul complains of himself in Rom. 7 and Gal. 5.

9. This weakness, though, the Lord does not reckon against His elect, for the sake of the Lord Christ, as is written, "There is now nothing accursed in those who are in Christ Jesus." Rom. 8.

10. We also believe, teach and confess, that not our works, but only the Spirit of God, of whose presence and indwelling through faith good works are witnesses, preserves faith and salvation.

NEGATIVE

False contrary teaching

1. Accordingly, we reject and damn speaking in this way, when it is taught and written that good works are necessary for salvation. Likewise, that no one has ever been saved without good works. Likewise, that it is impossible to be saved without good works.
Georg Major taught this error in Wittenberg.

2. We reject and damn this bare saying as offensive and disadvantageous to Christian conduct, when it is said, "Good works are damaging to salvation."
With this false sentence, Nikolaus Amsdorf came into the dispute.
For especially in these last times it is not less necessary to admonish and remind the people to Christian conduct and good works than it is necessary to show their faith and gratitude to God in the practice of good works: that works not be mixed into the article on justification, because the people can be damned as well through Epicurean craziness about faith as through a Papistic and Pharisaic trust in one's own works and merits.

3. We also reject and damn when it is taught that faith and indwelling of the Holy Spirit are not lots through deliberate sin, but that the saints and elect retain the Holy Spirit even when they fall

into and persist in adultery and other sin.

This was an error of Johann Agricola of Eisleben and all Antinomians (people who attack the Law), as well as strict Calvinists, who assert that an elect person cannot entirely lose faith, spirit and God's grace even through deadly sins.

V
Of the Law and Gospel

STATUS OF THE CONTROVERSY

The chief question in this dispute

Whether the preaching of the holy Gospel is actually not only a preaching of grace, which proclaims the forgiveness of sins, but also a preaching of penitence and punishment, which condemns unbelief which is not condemned by the Law, but is condemned solely by the Gospel.

AFFIRMATIVE

Pure teaching of God's Word

1. We believe, teach and confess that the distinction of Law and Gospel is to be maintained with great diligence in the churches as a particularly splendid light, through which the Word of God is rightly divided according to the admonition of St. Paul.

2. We believe, teach and confess that the Law is actually a divine teaching, which teaches what is right and pleasing to God and condemns everything that is sin and contrary to God's will.

3. Therefore, then, everything that condemns sin is and belongs to the preaching of the Law.

4. The Gospel however is actually a doctrine that teaches what a person who has not upheld the Law and is thereby damned should believe, namely that Christ has atoned for and paid for all sin, and has attained for him[57], without any merit of his own, forgiveness of sins, righteousness that is valid before God, and eternal life.

5. Since however the word Gospel is not used in only one sense in the holy Scripture, this dispute has arisen, so we believe, teach and confess, when the word Gospel is understood to mean the entire

---
[57]Tr. note: the sinner.

teaching of Christ, which He, in His teaching office set forth, as also His apostles (in which sense it is used in Mark 1 and Acts 20), then it is rightly said that the Gospel is a preaching of repentance and forgiveness of sins.

6. When, however, the Law and Gospel, as Moses himself, as a teacher of the Law, and Christ as a preacher of the Gospel are held up against each other: we believe, teach and confess that the Gospel is not a preaching of penitence or condemnation but actually nothing other than a preaching of consolation and a joyful message, that neither condemns nor terrifies, but rather consoles consciences against the terror of the Law, points only to the merit of Christ, and restores them with the loving preaching of the grace and favor of God, attained through Christ's merit.

7. As far as the revealing of sin, because the veil of Moses hangs in front of the eyes of all people, as long as they only hear the bare preaching of the Law and nothing of Christ, and thus do not learn to recognize their sin properly from the Law, but either become presumptuous hypocrites like the Pharisees or despair like Judas, then Christ takes the Law in his hands and presents it spiritually, Matt. 5; Rom. 7. And so God's wrath from heaven is revealed upon all sinners, how great the same is, through which they are sent to the Law, and only then, from the same, learn to recognize their sin, which recognition Moses would never have been able to force out of them.

After that, although the preaching of the suffering and death of Christ, the Son of God, is an earnest and terrifying preaching and demonstration of God's wrath, through which the people learn only then, after the veil of Moses has been taken away from then, how great a thing God demands of us in the Law, of which we can keep nothing, and after that should seek all our righteousness in Christ:

8. However, as long as all this (namely Christ's suffering and death) preaches God's wrath and terrifies people, it is still not yet the actual preaching of the Gospel, but a preaching of Moses and the Law and accordingly a work foreign to Christ, through which he comes to his own office, which is to preach grace, comfort and make alive, which is really the preaching of the Gospel.

NEGATIVE

Contrary teaching, hence rejected

Accordingly, we reject and consider it as false and harmful, when it is taught, that the Gospel is actually a preaching of penitence or punishment and not solely a preaching of grace, so that the Gospel becomes again a teaching of Law, the merit of Christ and holy Scripture are hidden, the Christians are robbed of true comfort, and the door is reopened to the papacy.

VI
Of the Third Use of the Law

STATUS OF THE CONTROVERSY

The main question of this dispute

Since the Law was given to people for three causes, first that through it outward behavior is kept from wild disobedience, second that people through it are led to recognition of their sins, third after they are regenerated, and yet the flesh still hangs onto them, that they for the same reason have a certain rule, according to which they can set up and govern their life, a division arose between a few theologians over the third use of the Law, whether namely such a thing is to be pushed at the regenerate Christians. One party said Yes, the other, No.

AFFIRMATIVE

The right Christian teaching of this dispute

1. We believe, teach and confess that although the people who are orthodox and truly converted to God have been freed and made independent of the Law's curse and compulsion, they ought not for that reason to be lawless, but because they have been redeemed by the Son of God, that they should exercise themselves in the same day and night (Ps. 119). Our first parents, in whose hearts God's Law was written, did not live without a Law before the Fall, because they had been created in God's image.

2. We believe, teach and confess that the preaching of the Law is to be conducted diligently not only with the unbelievers and impenitent, but also among those who are orthodox, truly converted, regenerate and justified by faith.

3. For although they are regenerate and renewed in spirit,[58] such rebirth and renewal is not complete in this world, but only begun,

---

[58] Walther's *"im Geist ihres Gemüts"* would be translated literally "in the spirit of their spirit," because there are two different German words that signify different things that are translated with the same word in English. It is simpler, clearer and better English as translated.

and the faithful are, with their spirit, in a constant battle against the flesh, against the corrupted nature and way that stays with us until death. Because of this old Adam, which still sticks to the understanding, will, and all powers of a person, in order that they not, out of human devotion, undertake services to God of their own will and choosing, it is necessary that the Law of the Lord always enlighten them, likewise, that the old Adam not use his own will, but be compelled to follow the Spirit and surrender himself against his will, not only with the admonitions and threats of the Law, but also with the rebukes and punishments.

4. As far as the difference between the works of the Law and the fruits of the spirit, we believe, teach and confess that works that happen according to the Law, as long as they are, and are called, works of the Law, are only forced out of people by the teaching of the rebukes and threats of God's wrath.

5. Fruits of the spirit, however, which the Spirit of God, which lives in the faithful, works through the regenerate, and are done by the faithful, as far as they are regenerate, as if they knew of no commandment, threat or reward—in that form, then, the children of God live and walk according to the Law of God, which St. Paul in his epistles, calls the law of the Spirit and the law of Christ.

6. Thus the Law is and remains, both with the penitent and the impenitent, with regenerate and unregenerate people, a single Law, namely the unchangeable will of God, and the difference is, concerning obedience, only in the person, for one, who is not yet regenerate, does what is demanded of him only by compulsion and unwillingly (as also the regenerate according to the flesh); the believer, however, does without compulsion with a willing spirit, as far as he is regenerate, what no threats of the Law can ever force out of him again.

False Contrary Teaching

Accordingly, we reject as a harmful error, contrary to Christian conduct and true Godliness, when it is taught that the Law should be taught in the above-reported way and extent only to the unbelieving, non-Christians, and unrepentant, and not to Christians and orthodox believers.

Error of Agricola and his adherents, the Antinomians or attackers of the Law.

VII
Of Christ's Holy Supper

Although the Zwinglian teachers are not to be counted among the theologians related to the Augsburg Confession, as they set themselves apart right at that time when that Confession was delivered, however, because they want to push their way in and place their error under the name of that same Christian confession, we wanted to make a necessary report on this division.

The Zwinglians only wanted to be related to the Augsburg Confession in order to participate in the benefits of the religious peace, and to be able to smuggle their teachings into the Lutheran Church.

STATUS OF THE CONTROVERSY

The Chief Dispute between Our Doctrine and that of the Sacramentarians in this article

Whether in the Holy Supper the true Body and Blood of our Lord Jesus Christ is truly and substantially present, distributed with bread and wine, and received with the mouth by all those who use this Sacrament, be they worthy or unworthy, pious or impious, believing or unbelieving, to the comfort and life of believers, to the judgment of the unbelievers? The Sacramentarians say no, we say yes.

In explaining this dispute it is to be noted at the beginning that there are two sorts of Sacramentarians. Some are gross Sacramentarians, who with plain, clear words state what they hold in their heart, that in the Holy Supper nothing is present except bread and wine, distributed and received with the mouth. Some however are sly and the most damaging Sacramentarians, who speak in partapparently with our own words and claim they also believe a true presence of the true, substantial, living Body and Blood of Christ in the Holy Supper, but this occurs spiritually through faith. This, under these plausible words, really retains exactly the first, gross meaning, that namely nothing is present and received by the mouth but bread and wine.

For "spiritual" means for them nothing other than that the spirit of Christ, or the power of the absent body of Christ and his merit, is present; the body of Christ, however is in no manner or way present, but only above in the highest heaven, to which we with the thoughts of our faith raise ourselves, and only there, but absolutely not in the bread and wine of the Supper, should seek the Body and Blood.

AFFIRMATIVE

Confession of the true doctrine of the holy Supper against the Sacramentarians

1. We believe, teach and confess that in the holy Supper the Body and Blood of Christ are truly and substantially present, and are truly distributed and received in the bread and wine.

2. We believe, teach and confess, that the words of the Testament of Christ are not otherwise to be understood than as they appear literally, that the bread and wine do not signify the absent Body and Blood of Christ, but that through the sacramental union they are the Body and Blood of Christ.

3. Concerning the consecration, we believe, teach and confess that such presence of the Body and Blood in the holy Supper is not done by the work or speech of a certain person, but that such is solely and alone to be ascribed to the almighty power of our Lord Jesus Christ.

4. Besides that, however, we also believe, teach and confess unanimously that in the use of the holy Supper the words of the institution of Christ are in no way to be omitted, but should be spoken openly, as it is written: "The blessed chalice, which we bless," etc., 1 Cor. 11. This blessing occurs through the speaking of the words of Christ.

5. The ground, however, on which we stand against the Sacramentarians in this matter are, as Dr. Luther has written in his great confession:[59]

The first is this article of our Christian faith: Jesus Christ is true, substantial, natural, full God and man, in one person not separated and undivided.

The second: that God's right hand is everywhere, at which Christ, according to His human nature, in fact and truth seated, is present, rules, and has in his hands and under his feet everything that is in heaven and on earth, where otherwise no person or angel, but only the Son of Mary, from where he also can do such things.

The third: that God's Word is not false or a lie.

The fourth: that God has many ways and knows, how to be at a place, and not only the one which the philosophers call local or spatial.

6. We believe, teach and confess that the Body and Blood of

---

[59] Martin Luther, *Confession Concerning Christ's Supper* (LW 37:214).

Christ are not only spiritually through faith, but also orally, though not in a Capernaitic, but in a supernatural, heavenly way, through the sacramental union, and are received with the bread and wine, as the words of Christ clearly express it, for Christ says, "take, eat, and drink," as then happened with the Apostles; for it is written, "And they all drank from it." Mark 14. Of the same, St. Paul says: "The bread that we break is a fellowship of the Body of Christ," that is: Whoever eats this bread, eats the Body of Christ; which the leading ancient teachers of the Church all witness: Chrysostom, Cyprian, Leo I, Gregory, Ambrose, and Augustine.

7. We believe, teach and confess that not only the rightly believing and worthy, but also the unworthy and unbelieving receive the true Body and Blood of Christ, though not to life and comfort, but to judgment and damnation, when they do not convert and repent.

For even if they reject Christ as a Savior, they must still, against their will, admit him as a stern Judge, who thus present exercises and shows His judgment in the unrepentant guests, as at the same time He works life and comfort in the hearts of the believing and worthy guests.

8. We also believe, teach and confess that there is only one kind of unworthy guests, namely those who do not believe, of whom it is written: "But whoever does not believe, he is already judged," which judgment is compounded and made greater and heavier by unworthy use of the Sacrament. 1 Cor. 11.

9. We believe, teach and confess that no believer, as long as he retains a living faith, receives the holy Supper to his judgment, as it has been instituted especially for weakly-believing yet repentant Christians for comfort and strengthening of their weak faith.

10. We believe, teach and confess that all worthiness of the guests at the table of this heavenly Supper is and stands alone in the holiest obedience and complete merit of Christ, which we appropriate to ourselves through true faith and which is secured to us through the Sacrament, and absolutely not in our virtues or inward or outward preparations.

NEGATIVE

Contrary condemned teaching of the Sacramentarians

On the other hand, we reject and condemn unanimously all the following erroneous articles, which are opposed and contrary to the doctrine, simple faith and confession of the Lord's Supper which has just been set forth:

1. The papal transubstantiation, which is taught in the papacy, that bread and wine in the holy Supper lose their substance and

natural being and thus become nothing, that it is transformed into the Body of Christ and only the outward form remains.

2. The papal sacrificial Mass for the sins of the living and the dead.

3. That the laity are given only one form of the Sacrament and, against the open Word of Christ's Testament, the chalice is withheld from them and they are robbed of his Blood.

This is well known to happen in the Roman church.

4. When it is taught that the words of the Testament of Christ should not be understood or believed simply, but that they are dark speeches, the understanding of which one should seek elsewhere.

Thus taught the Zwinglians and Calvinists.

5. That the Body of Christ in the holy Supper is not received orally with the bread, but that only bread and wine are received orally, and the Body of Christ is received spiritually through faith.

6. That bread and wine in the holy Supper are nothing more than signs by which Christians recognize each other.

7. That bread and wine are only symbols, likenesses and portrayals of the far absent Body and Blood of Christ.

The teachings under numbers 5,6 and 7 are likewise erroneous teachings of the Zwinglians and Calvinists.

8. That bread and wine are not more than memorials, seals and pledges, through which we are assured, when faith lifts itself into heaven, that it will then truly become a participant in the Body and Blood of Christ, as truly as we eat bread and wine in the holy Supper.

Teaching of Calvin and his adherents.

9. That the assurance and confirmation of our faith in the holy Supper happens solely through the outward signs of bread and wine, and not through the truly present Body and Blood of Christ.

10. That in the holy Supper only the power, effect and merit of the absent Body and Blood of Christ are distributed.

The teachings numbered 9 and 10 are likewise erroneous teachings of Calvin and his adherents.

11. That the body of Christ is so enclosed in heaven that he cannot in any way ever be at many or all places on earth at the same time, where his holy Supper is celebrated.

Teaching of the Calvinists and Crypto-Calvinists.

12. That Christ cannot have promised, nor accomplished, the substantial presence of his Body and Blood in the holy Supper, because the nature and properties of his assumed human nature cannot bear or permit such a thing.

Teaching of Peter Martyr, Beza, and other Calvinists.

13. That God, according to all His omnipotence (what a horrible thing to hear) cannot manage it that his body could be present at

more than one place at one time.

Like number 12.

14. That not the almighty words of the Testament of Christ, but faith forms and makes the presence of the Body and Blood of Christ in the holy Supper.

Teaching of the enthusiast Schwenkfeld in Silesia and the Zwinglians.

15. That the faithful should not seek the Body of Christ in the bread and wine of the holy Supper, but should lift up their eyes from the bread to heaven and seek the Body of Christ there.

Teaching of Calvin and his adherents.

16. That the unbelieving and unrepentant Christians do not receive the true Body and Blood of Christ, but only bread and wine.

Like number 15.

17. That the worthiness of the guests by this heavenly meal consists not only of true faith in Christ, but also on a person's outward preparation.

Teaching of Peter Martyr and other Calvinists.

18. That also true believers, who have and retain a true, living and pure faith in Christ can receive this Sacrament to their judgment because they have not completely changed outwardly.

Teaching of Bucer in Strassburg and a few Calvinists.

19. That the outward, visible elements of bread and wine in the holy Sacrament should be worshiped.

Teaching of the Papists.

20. In the same way we commend to the just judgment of God all joking, mocking, blasphemous questions (for the sake of decency not to be repeated here) and sayings about a gross, carnal, Capernaitic and repulsive manner that the Sacramentarians have propounded blasphemously and infuriatingly of the supernatural, heavenly secrets of this Sacrament.

Meant here are horrible sayings of Zwingli, Beza and other Calvinists.

21. We condemn and hold against the Capernaitic eating of the Body of Christ, as if one ripped his Body with teeth and digested like food, which the Sacramentarians, against their own consciences, over all sorts of evidence, press onto us willfully and make our doctrine, in that form, hateful to their hearers. Against that, we hold to the simple words of the Testament of Christ, a true, though supernatural, eating of the Body of Christ, likewise drinking of his Blood, which human mind and reason cannot comprehend, but our understanding in obedience to Christ, as in all articles of faith, is captured, and such a secret is not grasped otherwise than by faith and revealed in the Word.

The eating of the Body of Christ, as if the same were

ripped apart by the teeth, is called Capernaitic because the people of Capernaum misunderstood Christ's words about the spiritual eating of His flesh. John 6:53-63.

VIII
Of the Person of Christ

Out of the dispute about the holy Supper, a disunity has arisen between the pure theologians of the Augsburg Confession and the Calvinists (who have also caused some other theologians to err) over the person of Christ, of the two natures in Christ, and their properties.

STATUS OF THE CONTROVERSY
Main Dispute in this Division

The chief question is, however, whether the divine and human natures, for the sake of the personal union, really, in deed and truth, as well as their properties, have communion together, and how far such communion extends.

The Sacramentarians have suggested that the divine and human natures in Christ are united in such a way that neither really has the properties of the other, but have only the name in common. For union, they say simply, creates a common name, that is, the personal union makes nothing more than the name in common, that namely God is called man and man God, in such a way that God has nothing in common with mankind, and mankind nothing with the Godhead and its majesty and attributes in reality, that is, in deed and truth. Dr. Luther and those who held with him have argued the opposite.

AFFIRMATIVE

Pure teaching of the Christian churches of the Person of Christ

To clarify this dispute and, guided by our Christian faith, to set it aside, our teaching, belief and confession is as follows:

1. That the divine and human natures in Christ are personally united, hence, that there are not two Christs, one God's, the other man's, son, but there is one single Son of God and Son of Man. Luke 1; Rom. 9.

2. We believe, teach and confess that the divine and human natures are not mixed into a single essence, neither transformed

into the other, but each retains its essential properties, which never become attributes of the other nature.

3. The properties of divine nature are: almighty, eternal, unending, according to the property of the nature and its natural essence, for itself, present everywhere, knowing everything, etc., which never become the properties of the human nature.

4. The properties of human nature are: to be a physical creation or creature, to be flesh and blood, ending and finite, to suffer, to die, to ascend and descend, to move from one place to the other, to suffer hunger, thirst, frost, heat, and the like, which never become properties of the divine nature.

5. Since both natures are personally united, that is, in one person: we believe, teach and confess that this union is not such a knitting and connecting together that neither nature should have anything in common personally, that is, for the sake of the personal union, with the other, as when someone glues two boards together, where neither gives or receives anything from the other. Rather, it is the highest community that God has with a person, from which personal union and the resultant highest and unspeakable communion, everything flows to us, what is said and believed humanly about God and divinely about people. The old church teachers explained this through a comparison to a glowing iron, as also the union of body and soul in a person.

6. Therefore we believe, teach and confess that [in Christ] God is man, and man God, which could not be, if the divine and human natures had nothing in common with each other at all.

For how could the man, Mary's son, be called or be truly God or the Son of the Most High God, if his humanity were not really personally united, in deed and truth, but had only a name God in common with God's Son?

7. Therefore we believe, teach and confess that Mary did not receive and bear a mere, simple man, but the true Son of God; therefore she is also rightly called, and is, the Mother of God.

8. Therefore we also believe, teach and confess that not a mere, simple man suffered, died, was buried, descended to hell, rose from the dead, ascended into heaven and was seated with the majesty and almighty power of God, but such a person that is in such a deep, unspeakable union and communion with the Son of God, that they are in him one person.

9. Therefore truly the Son of God suffered for us, though according to the property of the human nature which he took on in union with his divine person and made him his own, that he could suffer and be our high priest for our reconciliation with God, as is written: "They have crucified the Lord of glory." And: "With God's blood, we have been redeemed." 1 Cor. 2; Acts 20.

10. Therefore we believe, teach and confess that the Son of Man has really, in deed and truth, been raised to the right of the almighty majesty and power of God, because he was, through the Holy Ghost, received into his mother's body and his human nature was united with the Son of the Most High.

11. Which majesty he has always had through the personal union and yet placed himself outside it in the state of his humiliation and by that reason gained all wisdom and favor with God and people. Therefore he showed this majesty not all the time, but when it pleased him, until he completely set aside the form of a slave, and not the nature, after his resurrection and entered into the full use, revelation and demonstration of the divine majesty and thus into his glory, that he, not only as God but as man, knows everything, can do everything, is present to all creatures, and has everything that is in heaven, on earth, and under the earth, under his feet and in his hands, as he himself testifies: "I have been given all power in heaven and on earth." And St. Paul: "He is ascended above all heaven, that he fulfilled everything." He can exercise this power of his everywhere, and all things are possible and knowable to him.

12. Therefore he can, and it is quite easy for him, to be present and communicate his true Body and Blood in the holy Supper, not according to the way or property of his human nature, but according to the way or property of His divine rights, says Doctor Luther from our Christian children's faith, which presence is not earthly, nor Capernaitic, yet true and substantial, as the words of his testament say, "This, is, is, is my Body," etc..

Through this teaching, belief and confession of ours, the person of Christ is not divided as Nestorius did (who denied the communication of attributes, that is, the true community of the properties of both natures in Christ, and thereby divided the person, as Luther explains in the book on the Councils); nor are the natures, with all their properties mixed together in a single essence (as Eutyches erred); nor the human nature concealed in the person of Christ, nor erased away; nor is either nature changed into the other; but Christ is and remains in all eternity God and man in one undivided person, which is, after the holy Trinity the highest secret, as the apostle testifies, in which our eternal comfort, life and salvation stands.

NEGATIVE

Contrary False Doctrine of the Person of Christ

Accordingly, we reject and condemn as contrary to God's Word and our simple Christian faith all the following erroneous articles, when it is taught:

1. That God and man in Christ are not one person, but one Son of God and another Son of Man, as Nestorius blathered.

Nestorius was a heretic, whose erroneous doctrine was condemned at the third general council at Ephesus in 431.

2. That the divine and human natures are mingled in one essence, and the human nature has been changed into the Godhead, as Eutyches raved.

Eutyches was a heretic, whose erroneous teaching was condemned at the fourth general council at Chalcedon in 451.

3. That Christ is not true, natural, eternal God, as Arius held.

Arius was a heretic, who was condemned at the first general council at Nicaea in 325.

4. That Christ did not have a true human nature, as Marcion made up.

Marcion was a heretic who appeared in the second century.

5. That the personal union makes only a common title and name.

Teaching of the Zwinglians, Crypto-Calvinists and Jesuits.

6. That it is only a phrase and a way of speaking when one says, "God is man; man is God [in Christ]"; for the divinity really has nothing in common with the humanity, as also the humanity with the divinity.

Like number 5.

7. That it is nothing but words when it is said that God's Son die for the sins of the world, the Son of Man became almighty.

Like number 5.

8. That the human nature in Christ has become an unending essence on the same basis as the divinity and is everywhere present from an essential power and property that has been given and poured into the human nature and separated from God.

This error is expressly rejected because the Zwinglians, Calvinists and Crypto-Calvinists, contrary to the truth, accused the orthodox Lutherans, especially those in Württemberg, of this error, in order to make the pure teaching of the person of Christ suspect and to cloak their own erroneous doctrine.

9. That the human nature has become equal and like to the divine nature in its substance and essence or in their essential properties.

Like number 8.

10. That the human nature of Christ is spatially extended into all parts of heaven and earth, which is not even given to the divine nature.

Like number 8.

11. That it is impossible for Christ, because of the properties of his human nature, to be at more than one place at one time, much less to be everywhere with his Body.

Teaching of the Calvinists, especially of Beza and Peter Martyr.

12. That only the bare humanity [of Christ] suffered for us and redeemed us, and that the Son of God has nothing to do with the suffering, as if it had not happened to him.

Teaching of Zwingli and the Calvinists.

13. That Christ is only with us on earth in Word, Sacrament and all our needs according to his divinity, and such presence has nothing to do with his human nature, according to which he, after his suffering and death redeemed us, has nothing more to do.

14. That the Son of God, having assumed the human nature, after he laid aside the form of a slave, does not accomplish all the works of his omnipotence in, through and with his human nature, but only a few, and only at the place where the human nature is spatially.

15. That he is not capable according to the human nature of the omnipotence and other attributes of the divine nature in all things, contrary to the express saying of Christ: "All power has been given me in heaven and on earth." And St. Paul: "In him dwells the whole fullness of the Godhead bodily." Col. 2.

16. That greater power was given him in heaven and on earth, namely greater and more than all angels and other creatures, but he has nothing in common with the omnipotence of God, the same not having been given to him. Hence they invent a middle power, that is, a power between God's omnipotent power and the power of other creatures, which has been given to Christ according to his human nature through the Ascension, which is less than God's almighty power and greater than the power of other creatures.

17. That Christ, according to his human spirit, has a certain amount that he should know, and that he does not know more than is fitting to him and is necessary to know for his office as judge.

18. That Christ does not yet have a full knowledge of God and of all his works, though it is written of this: "that in him all treasures of wisdom and of knowledge are hidden."

19. That it is impossible for Christ according to his human spirit to know what happened from eternity, what is happening everywhere now, and what will yet happen in eternity.

Also the teachings under numbers 13-19 are teachings of Zwingli and the Calvinists.

20. When it is taught and the saying of Matt. 28: "All power has been given me," etc., is interpreted and blasphemously distorted to mean that Christ according to his human nature was restored, that

is, all power in heaven and on earth were given back to him as if he had in his state of humiliation also laid this aside and abandoned it also according to his divinity. Through this teaching, not only the words and testament of Christ are distorted, but also the way of the damned heresy of Arius is prepared, that ultimately denies Christ's eternal divinity and thus Christ lost all our salvation, since such false teaching would not be contradicted on the firm ground of God's Word and our simple Christian faith.

Teaching of the Calvinists and Crypto-Calvinists, according to which they asserted that Christ lowered himself according to both natures, hence according to the divine, with which they made God into a changeable being, against God's clear Word. Ps. 102:28.

IX
Of Christ's Descent Into Hell

STATUS OF THE CONTROVERSY

Main Dispute over this Article

It has also been disputed among some theologians who contributed to the Augsburg Confession, when and in what manner the Lord Christ, according to our simple Christian faith, descended into hell, whether it happened before or after his death. Likewise, whether it was only his soul, or only his divinity, or with body and soul, spiritually of physically. Also, whether this article belongs to the suffering or to the glorious victory and triumph of Christ.

Since however this article, like the previous one, cannot be comprehended with the mind nor with reason, but must be grasped solely by faith, it is our unanimous consideration not to dispute this, but should only be believed and taught in the simplest way; as the blessed Dr. Luther in the sermon at Torgau in 1533 and elsewhere explains it in a quite Christian way, with all useless, unnecessary questions cut away and admonishing all pious Christians to Christian simplicity.

For it is enough that we know that Christ descended into hell, destroyed hell for all believers, and redeemed them from the power of death, devil, eternal damnation and the jaws of hell. As it has happened, however, we should leave to the next world, when not just this thing but other ones will be revealed to us that we have here only believed and cannot comprehend with our blind reason.

In the second part of the Formula of Concord, which contains the comprehensive explanation of the first part, it is confessed expressly as the teaching of our church about Christ's descent into hell, "that the whole person, God and man, descended after the burial innto heaven, vanquished the devil, destroyed the power of hell and took from the devil all his might." Through this confession, our church rejects those who believe and teach that Christ only descended with his soul to hell, or that the descent to hell should be taken figuratively and only understood to be Christ's last sufferings, or his death, or his burial, or, that Christ in hell suffered the pain of the damned, that therefore the descent into hell of Christ is not to be counted to his triumph but to his state of humiliation.

X
Of Church Customs which one calls Adiaphora or Middle Things

Of ceremonies or church customs, which are neither commanded nor forbidden in God's Word, but have been introduced into the Church for the sake of good order and well-being, a division emerged between the theologians of the Augsburg Confession.

STATUS OF THE CONTROVERSY

The Correct, True Teaching and Confession of this Article

1. Toward resolution of this dispute as well, we believe, teach and confess unanimously that the ceremonies or church customs which are neither commanded nor forbidden in God's Word but instituted solely for the sake of well-being and good order are of themselves no service of God nor any part thereof. Matt. 15: "They honor me uselessly with human commandments."

2. We believe, teach and confess that the congregation of God in every place and every time has the freedom on any occasion to alter such ceremonies, as it may be most useful and edifying to the congregation of God.

Here the freedom to decide all things that God has neither commanded nor forbidden that affect the Church is assured to every single congregation of all

places and times.

3. However, in this all frivolity and offense should be avoided, and especially the weak in faith should be spared with all diligence.

4. We believe, teach and confess that at the time of persecution, when a full confession is required of us, we should not yield to enemies in such middle things, as the apostle wrote: "So stand firm now in freedom, with which Christ has freed us, and do not let yourselves be caught again in the yoke of slavery." Again: "Do not pull a strange yoke; what has the light in common with the darkness?" Again: "That the truth of the Gospel might remain with you, we did not yield to them [even] one hour, to be subject to them."

For in such a case, it is no longer about middle things, but about the truth of the Gospel, about Christian freedom and about ratifying public idolatry, as well as prevention of offending the weak in faith, in which we have nothing to concede, but should fully confess and suffer therefor what God has sent us and granted to the enemies of His Word against us.

5. We believe, teach and confess also that no church should condemn the other, that one has fewer or more outward ceremonies that God has not commanded than the other, when there is otherwise unity between them in doctrine and all of the same articles, as well as in the right use of the Sacraments, following the well-known saying: "Inequality in fasting should not divide unity in faith."

Our church calls here for the Church's unity in all articles of Christian doctrine.

NEGATIVE

False Teaching on this Article

Accordingly we reject and condemn it as wrong and contrary to God's Word, when it is taught:

1. That human commandments and rules should of themselves be held as divine services, or a part thereof.

Erroneous teaching of the papists.

2. When such ceremonies, commandments and rules are imposed upon God's congregation with force, as necessary, against its Christian freedom which it has in outward things.

Papal tyranny.

3. Also, that one, in a time of persecution and public confession, may comply with the enemies of the holy Gospel in such middle things and ceremonies (which serves to break from the truth), or compromise with them.

Erroneous teaching of the Philippists, that is, the blind admirers of Philipp Melanchthon, mainly in Elec-

toral Saxony, in that time when the Emperor wanted to impose the unionistic book, called Interim, on the Lutherans.

4. Also, when such outward ceremonies and middle things are abolished as if they should not be free to the congregation of God, on appropriate occasions, as it may be useful to the churches to use one or more of them in Christian freedom.

Erroneous teaching of the papists, as well as the Calvinists, who wanted to make many middle things a sin for the Lutherans.

XI
Of the Eternal Foreknowledge and Election of God

On this article, there has not been any public division among the theologians of the Augsburg Confession. However, because it is a comforting article, when it is rightly handled, and therefore, that in the future offensive disputes may not be introduced, it is also explained in this writing.

As meticulous as our faithful fathers were with the confession of this article in order to anticipate possible future disputes, we Lutherans should be just as meticulous at all times to preserve this good addendum.

AFFIRMATIVE

True, Pure Teaching of This Article

1. To begin with, the difference between foreknowledge and predestination, or the election of God, to be noted with diligence.

Calvin removes this distinction; he says, for example, it is unnecessary to dispute how God could know every thing in advance, since everything happens as God has determined beforehand. The Calvinist Reformed, for example the Presbyterians, follow him in this teaching.

2. For God's foreknowledge is nothing other than that God knows all things before they happen, as it is written: "God in heaven can reveal hidden things; he showed King Nebuchadnezzar what would happen in future times."

3. This foreknowledge goes over the pious and the wicked alike,

but is no cause of evil, nor of sins, that one does wrong (which originally comes from the devil and the perverted will of a person), nor their corruption, of which they are guilty themselves, but only puts all that in order, and sets an end, how long it should last, and without regard to that it is itself evil, that it should serve to the salvation of his elect.

>Zwingli, Calvin, and those who followed them taught the opposite, that God also knows the evil in advance because he has decided that it should happen.

4. Predestination, or the eternal election of God, applies only to the pious, pleasing children of God, and is a cause of their salvation, which he also created and ordered, by which our salvation is so firmly grounded that the gates of hell cannot overpower it.

>With this, not only is the erroneous teaching of the Calvinists that there is also a predestination to damnation, but also the teaching of the Pelagians, Semi-Pelagians and Synergists, that the salvation of a person is not founded on the gracious election of God, but that election and thus also salvation is based much more on the conduct and the decision of the person.

11. That, however, "many are called and few are chosen," does not have the meaning that God does not want to save everyone, but the reason is that either they do not hear God's Word at all, but willfully despise it, they stop their ears and their hearts, and so block the orderly way of the Holy Spirit so that he cannot do his work in them, or, since they have heard it, throw it back into the wind and pay no attention to it, for which not God or his election, but their own wickedness is responsible.

>The opposite is taught by the Calvinists, who assert that grace is irresistible and that whoever once stands in grace cannot fall back out of grace, but the cause why so many are not saved is God, because God does not want to save them.

12. And a Christian should accept the article of the eternal election of God as far as it is revealed in the Word of God, which Christ shows us as the book of life, which he, through preaching, opens and reveals, as it is written, "Those whom he elected, he also called," in which we should seek the eternal election of the Father, who in his eternal, divine counsel has decided that he does not want to save anyone other than those who recognize his Son Christ and truly believe in him. [They should] reject other thoughts, which flow here not from God but from the insertion of the evil foe, with

which he undertakes to weaken or even to take away completely the wonderful comfort that we have in this salutary doctrine: that we know how we are elected in Christ to eternal life out of pure grace and without any of our own merit; how he does not merely agree to such a gracious election with bare words, but also insists on it with a promise and has sealed it with the holy Sacraments, which we remember under the worst attacks and are comforted and can thereby quench the fiery arrows of the devil.

13. Besides that, we should be most diligent to live according to the will of God and, as St. Peter reminds us, "make our calling firm," and especially hold to the revealed Word; that cannot and will not fail us.

14. Through this short explanation of the eternal election of God, God is given his whole and full honor, that he alone, out of sheer mercy without any merit of ours, saves us according to the decree of his will, and no one is given any reason for faintheartedness or to raw, wild living.

Through the Pelagian teaching of predestination, God is robbed of his honor and it is given to man.

ANTITHESIS or NEGATIVE

False Teaching about This Article

Therefore, we believe and hold: those who so teach the doctrine of the gracious election of God to eternal life that alarmed Christians cannot be comforted by it, but through it are moved to faintheartedness and despair, or the unrepentant are affirmed in their willfulness, such doctrine is not driven by the Word and will of God, but by the reason and instigation of the miserable Satan. For all that is written, as the apostle testifies, "is written for our instruction, that we have hope, through patience and comfort of the Scripture." Accordingly, we reject the following errors:

Calvin himself says of predestination as he teaches it: "I admit, it is a terrifying counsel," with which he himself admits that his teaching is not evangelical, but is an invention of men that leads either to despair or to carnal security.

1. When it is taught that God does not want that all people repent and believe the Gospel.
Error of the Calvinist-Reformed.
2. Likewise, when God calls us to himself, he does not mean seriously that all people should come to him.
Like number 1.
3. Likewise, that God does not want that everyone be saved but,

without regard to their sin, solely through the bare counsel, decree and will of God, that they be ordered to damnation, that they cannot be saved.

Like number 1.

4. Likewise, that not only the mercy of God and the most holy merit of Christ, but also in us is a cause of the election of God, for the sake of which God has elected us to eternal life.

> **Error 1. of the Papists, who teach that the elect have been chosen for the sake of their good works which God has foreseen; 2. of the Synergists, who teach that the elect have been chosen for the sake of their faith, which God has foreseen, or for the sake of their cooperation or decision. For though it is true that God has elected only those of whom he saw in advance that they would believe to the end, it is false that he elected them because he foresaw that, otherwise election would not be an election of grace.**

All these are blasphemous, erroneous and terrifying doctrines, through which all comfort is taken from Christians that they have in the holy Gospel and use of the holy Sacraments, and because of that should not be tolerated in the churches of God.

This is the short and simple explanation of the disputed articles that were for a while debated and controverted among the theologians of the Augsburg Confession. From it every simple Christian according to the direction of God's Word and his simple catechism can detect what is right or wrong, since not only is the pure doctrine set forth, but also the contrary erroneous doctrine is excluded and rejected, and thus the distressing divisions that have occurred are decided thoroughly.

The almighty God and Father of our Lord Jesus grant the grace of his Holy Ghost, that we all be united in him and remain permanently in a unity pleasing to him. Amen.

XII
Of Other Factions and Sects That Never Acknowledged the Augsburg Confession

That the following not be silently ascribed to us, because we have not mentioned them [the other sects] in the foregoing explanation, we have at the end only wanted to tell of the articles in which they err and teach counter to our much-considered Christian faith and confession.

Erroneous Articles of the Anabaptists

The Anabaptists are divided among themselves into many groups [heaps], because some propound many, others few, errors; in general, however, they promote such doctrine as is neither to be tolerated in the churches nor in the police and secular government nor in homes.

> The sect of the Re-baptizers, or Anabaptists, or Baptists[60] as they are now called, is splintered into a great many parties which are distinguished from each other by wildly varying errors, but all are united in rejecting infant baptism. At the time of Luther, this sect appeared first in Zwickau, in Saxony, under Thomas Münzer, and after 1533 in Münster, in Westphalia, under J. Bockhold, called Johannes von Leyden, where they practiced the most horrifying abominations.

Intolerable Articles in the Churches

1. That Christ did not receive his body and blood from the Virgin Mary, but brought them with him from heaven.

2. That Christ is not truly God, but only has more gifts of the Holy Ghost than another holy man.

3. That our righteousness before God stands not only on the sole merit of Christ, but in renewal, and thus in our own piety in which we walk. Much of this is placed in their own, self-chosen spirituality, and is basically nothing more than a new monkery.

4. That children who are not baptized are not sinners before God, but are righteous and innocent, and are saved without baptism (which, according to their pretensions, they do not need) , because they have not yet come to understanding. Thus they reject the entire doctrine of original sin and everything that stems from it.

> They denied that unbaptized children are saved through an extraordinary working of grace; instead, they taught that unbaptized children were saved because they died in their innocence. It is not rejected here that the unbaptized children of Christians are saved, because we Lutherans believe that, too.

---

[60]The Anabaptists were the precursors of the Mennonites and Amish of today; the merger of some of their teachings with those of Calvinistic or Methodistic groups produced today's Baptists.

5. That children should not be baptized until they come to understanding and can confess their faith themselves.

6. That the children of Christians are, because they are born of Christian and believing parents, also holy and God's children; also, the cause of the baptism of children is neither held high nor promoted, contrary to the express words of the promise of God, that it extends only to those, "who keep his covenant and do not despise it." Gen. 17.

Also an error of the Calvinists.

7. That it is not a real Christian congregation, where sinners are found.

> **Was also the error of the old heretical Donatists in the fourth and fifth centuries. Compare Augsburg Confession Article 8.**

8. That one should not hear a sermon, nor visit in the temples where previously papal Mass was held and read.

9. That one should have nothing to do with the church ministers who preach according to the Augsburg Confession and preach against the Anabaptists and rebuke error, also not to serve them nor work for them, but flee them as perverters of God's Word and avoid them.

Intolerable Articles in Government

1. That rulers are not a God-pleasing class in the New Testament.

2. That a Christian cannot with a good, undamaged conscience cannot hold or administer the office of rule.

3. That a Christian cannot with an undamaged conscience use the office of rule in occasional matters against wicked ones, nor call upon the power, received from God, of its subordinates for defense and shelter.

4. That a Christian cannot with a good conscience swear any oath, nor swear fealty to his prince or ruler.

5.That rulers cannot in good conscience, under the New Testament, impose the death penalty on evildoers.

Intolerable Articles in Households

1. That a Christian cannot in good conscience retain or possess anything of his own, but is obligated to give it into the common use.

So these Anabaptists were Communists.

2. That a Christian cannot in good conscience be an innkeeper, merchant or cutler.

> **They say a Christian cannot be a cutler because he produces weapons of war.**

3. That married people may divorce for the sake of the faith and one may abandon the other and marry someone of his own faith.

Erroneous Articles of the Schwenkfelders
The founder of this sect was Caspar Schwenkfeld, from Ossigk in Silesia, born in 1562 in Ulm.

1. That those who regard Christ as a creature according to His flesh have no true knowledge of Christ, the reigning king of heaven.

Schwenkfeld believed on a "deification of the flesh of Christ," an error of which Lutherans were accused by the Calvinists, against all truth.

2. That the flesh of Christ, through his exaltation, has thus taken on all divine properties, that he, Christ, is as a man equal to the Father and the Word in might, strength, and majesty, that from now on Christ has a single substance, property, will and glory in both natures, and that the flesh of Christ now belongs to the substance of the Holy Trinity.

3. That the church service, the preached and heard Word, is not a means through which God the Holy Ghost teaches people the saving recognition of Christ, and works in them conversion, repentance, faith and new obedience.

Was also an error of Zwingli.

4. That the water of baptism is not a means through which God the Lord seals us as His children and works rebirth.

Is also an error of the Calvinistic-Reformed.

5. That bread and wine in the holy Supper are not means by which Christ distributes to us his body and blood.

Like number 4.

6. That a Christian who is truly reborn through the spirit of God can completely keep and fulfill the Law.

In this the Schwenkfelders agreed with the papists.

7. That it is no true Christian congregation where no public expulsion or orderly process of excommunication is maintained.

This was an error of the Donatists, who also asserted that a corrupted church is no church at all.

8. That a minister of the churches who is not personally renewed, reborn, just and pious cannot usefully teach others or administer true sacraments.

Like number 7.

Error of the new Arians

That Christ was not a true, substantial, natural God, of one eternal divine substance with God the Father and the Holy Ghost, but was only adorned with divine majesty, under and beside God the Father.

To these new Arians belonged, among others, Laelius Socinus and Faustus Socinus, two Italians. The later

attempted to spread his teaching first in Switzerland and later, after 1578, started the sect of the Socinians in Siebenbürgen[61] and Poland. A similar sect in this country is the Unitarians.[62]

Error of the Anti-Trinitarians

This is an entirely new sect, never before heard of in Christianity, who believe, teach and confess that there is not one single, eternal divine being, of the Father, Son and Holy Ghost, but as God Father, Son and Holy Ghost are three persons, so each person has his own distinct substance separate from the other persons of the Godhead. Either all three have, like three people different in their essence, equal power, wisdom, majesty and glory, or they are in their being and properties unequal, so that only the Father is the real, true God.

A person who denies the Trinity, that is, the mystery of the high, holy three in one, is called an Anti-Trinitarian. In this country, the Anti-Trinitarians are the Unitarians and the Swedenborgians.[63]

We reject and condemn these and similar articles and whatever else comes out of the same error and follows from it as untrue, false, heretical, and contrary to the Word of God, the three Creeds, the Augsburg Confession and Apology, the Smalcald Articles and the catechisms of Luther. All pious Christians of high or low estate should beware of them as they love their souls' well-being and salvation.

---

[61] Siebenbürgen was a region of Transylvania (western modern Romania) which was largely populated by Germans. Most of those Germans were expelled after World War 2.

[62] While there are still Unitarians in America today, by far the largest neo-Arian sect in the USA today is the Jehovah's Witnesses, or Watchtower Society.

[63] Again, this would include Jehovah's Witnesses. It would also include many of the purportedly Christian sects that have formed around television evangelists such as the Oneness Pentecostals and the "Word-Faith" movement of the likes of Kenneth and Gloria Copeland, Creflo Dollar, Benny Hinn and Joyce Meyer (who was raised a Lutheran and has absolutely no excuse for the heresies she teaches). All Lutherans, indeed, all Christians, should beware these wolves in sheep's clothing.

[Conclusion]

We have signed hereunder with full consideration, in true fear of God and calling upon him, with our own hands, that this is our whole teaching, belief and confession, as we intend to answer on the last day before the just Judge, our Lord Jesus Christ, and that we do not wish to say or write anything against it, either secretly or openly, but intend with the help of the grace of God to remain with it.

>Signed for the first time at Cloister Bergen near Magdeburg on May 29, 1577.

>Nikolaus Selnecker, in his description of the life of the Elector August of Saxony:

>"We can be certain that, as long as people in the churches and schools of this land and others hold to this confession and explanation, as it is contained in the Christian Book of Concord, orthodoxy without fanaticism in God's Word and doctrine, besides other blessings, with be and remain; as soon, however, as anyone departs in the least from the same true confession, God, who has given us this blessing, will depart from us and permit all sorts of blasphemy and fanaticism to break in among us."

>God preserve our dear American Lutheran church from that in grace; may he help, much more, that the Lord fulfill for her the promise of Rev. 3:10: "Since thou hast kept the Word of my patience, I also will keep thee from the hour of temptation, which shall come upon all the world to try them that dwell upon the earth."

>"Gottes Wort und Luthers Lehr
>Vergehet nun und nimmermehr."
>(God's Word and Luther's teaching
>Does not pass away now or ever.)

>Hallelujah!
>Amen!

The

Doctrine of Election

in

Questions and Answers

presented

From the eleventh article of the
Formula of Concord of the
Evangelical Lutheran Church

With a Preface and After-Word
by
C. F. W. Walther
Kenneth E. F. Howes, Translator

St. Louis, Mo.
Printed by the "Lutheran Concordia Publishing House"
1881

Translation © 2012 by Kenneth E.F. Howes

Preface

A short time ago, a treatise appeared in the "Lutheran Concordia Publishing House" at St. Louis, which bears the title, "The Dispute over the Doctrine of Election." At the end of this treatise, its author gave his readers the promise, that he would have a second treatise follow that one, in which he would present the pure Lutheran doctrine of election in the simplest way. The present little writing appears here in accord with that promise.

Whether the same is so composed as our readers wished and expected it is now, to be sure, the question.

Perhaps many would have preferred it if we had presented first the doctrine of election briefly and concisely in our own words. We believed, however, that we had first to take the answers to the questions put to us from our church confession, namely from the Formula of Concord, and for the following reasons: 1. because we really could not have answered the questions better; 2. because the Lutheran reader can most quickly be made certain exactly in this way, that the doctrine presented to him in this little book is not a new one, but is the old, pure doctrine of election of our orthodox Lutheran church; 3. because this way everyone who wants to see can see, that precisely the only true Lutheran doctrine of election is being rejected and cursed as godless Calvinistic heresy, and actually by men who want to be regarded as especially faithful Lutherans; 4. because in this way, by God's grace, it is ensured that this book does not also provoke dispute among confessional Lutherans; and 5. finally, because our confession itself says, that it has included the unanimous doctrine of our church on election, actually, "only to anticipate future disputes and divisions among our successors on this point."

Now, we already swore in Germany, 44 years ago at our ordination, a dear oath on the symbolic books of our church, by the salvation of our souls, to our church into whose service we entered, solemnly blessed, to be a true guardian of this precious property; we would therefore be an accursed oathbreaker, if we now, when people are screaming that the doctrine of our confession is Calvinism, are ashamed of our sworn confession, and do not want to bear all the disgrace that is heaped on us, so that we deny the same and, in our old age, as we have already come to the gates of eternity, fall away from it.

No, we would rather, because of our firm adherence to our confessions, go out of the world being called heretics and damned by people, and be received by God as His faithful stewards, by His grace, than die praised and made famous by people because we gave way, and then, like a rascally servant, hear from God, "I never knew you; go away from Me, you evildoer!"

We certainly know very well that not all who now call us heretics and damn us are un-Christian, but we are also, thank God! not the first who are, for the sake of the truth, called heretics and damned, even by Christians in their ignorance. When Jerome of Prague, on May 30, 1416, came to the stake, where he was to be burned for the sake of the truth, a little farmer came with a big bundle of twigs, to make his contribution, that the supposedly scandalous heretic would be put out of the world. The dear witness of the truth, Jerome of Prague, did not berate the little farmer, but called to him, with a smile, "O holy simpleness! The one who deceives you, he has a thousand times the sin." The holy martyr, however, also did not fall into doubt about his doctrine, for he saw, that even Christians, misled by others, joined in condemning him.

We, too, then, neither want to scold our deceived Christian opponents, nor to, for their sake, err from the truth, but remain with the confession of the truth, however it may go for us as a result. For to remain with the confession, when this brings praise and honor, is no art. When, however, for exactly that reason, one is declared to be disloyal, yes, as one who has fallen away from the confession, because one remains true to the Confession, that counts as passing the test and proving confessional faithfulness in deed.

Therefore if someone, like the papists, once more cries, "Fathers! Fathers!"—a true Lutheran then says, "God's Word and Luther's doctrine, do not pass away now or ever."[1] Perhaps, though, many think, if in this little writing, it's just about repeating the teaching of our Confession, namely our Formula of Concord, then it would have been enough if we had simply reprinted the eleventh article of the Formula of Concord. We only hope that the attentive reader will soon note that our questions do him good service.

He will notice that he can often too easily, in a mere skimming reading of the Formula of Concord, overlook just such points, which are of the highest importance. He now is made aware through these questions of these points. That is why earlier great theologians already put the whole Formula of Concord in the same way into question and answer. We can assure in good conscience that we, through our questions, have never gone out through our questions to stick foreign thoughts into our confession, but that we were solely of the intent only to bring teachings that are really contained in the same to light.

From a certain quarter, it has popped out that we earlier taught

---

[1] "Gottes Wort und Luther's Lehr-Vergehet nun und nimmermehr." (Slogan of the early Missouri Synod)

a doctrine of election different from the present one; this is, however, a gross falsehood, which we we could prove with the manuscripts of our sermons from the first time of our administration of the office in America, if it were necessary. It is just not worth the effort to do this, for if we earlier taught so or so of election, that has not the slightest to do with the question of which is the right teaching.

Luther also, in the year 1517, taught otherwise, when he posted the 95 Theses publicly, from ten years earlier, when he was ordained a priest, but his 95 Theses were not therefore false. Anyone who needs and brings such proofs to beat his opponent proves only that he must do that because he lacks real, cogent grounds. But, as said, as we teach today, so we have always taught, since God by marvelous guidings has brought us to a living recognition that God really, through the Lutheran Church Reformation, gave Christianity back the Christian doctrine in apostolic purity.

Perhaps many readers also hoped, the promised second treatise would present the doctrine of election in such a way that everything is removed that until now clashed with their reason or the reason of others. Now this is, I admit, not the case. But why not? Because such a presentation is not possible, if one does not want to falsify the doctrine of the holy Scripture and our Confession.

The holy Apostle Paul, as every diligent Bible reader knows, set forth the doctrine of election in the greatest detail in the 8th, 9th, 10th, and 11th chapters of his Epistle to the Romans, and what does he write at the close of his presentation? He calls out, "O what a depth of the riches, both of the wisdom and the knowledge of God! How incomprehensible are His judgments, and unsearchable his ways! For who has known the mind of the Lord? Or who has been His counselor? Or who has given Him something before, that is given back to Him? For from Him and through Him and to Him are all things. Honor be to Him eternally! Amen!"[2]

From this you see, dear reader: if these closing words of Paul do not fit with a presentation of the doctrine of election, if the presented doctrine does not move the reader also to cry out, "O how incomprehensible! O how unsearchable!" if the presentation agrees more nicely with reason—then it, to the contrary, certainly does not agree with the Holy Scripture and with the Scriptural confession

---

[2] Translation from the German text. The King James Version (the most applicable English form here, being, like Luther's, from the Received Text) has it:

33 O the depth of the riches both of the wisdom and knowledge of God! how unsearchable are his judgments, and his ways past finding out!
34 For who hath known the mind of the Lord? or who hath been his counsellor?
35 Or who hath first given to him, and it shall be recompensed unto him again?
36 For of him, and through him, and to him, are all things: to whom be glory for ever. Amen

of the orthodox Church; then it therefore contains a false doctrine mixed with human thoughts.

Do not be bothered, dear Lutheran reader, that we have not attempted in this little writing to present the doctrine of election in such a way that it fits in neatly with reason; but consider: this doctrine contains secrets that no human understanding in this life can fathom. Therefore, you must, as a faithful Lutheran Christian, as in all articles of faith, so also in this doctrine always just ask, "What is written?" and then take your reason captive under the obedience of Christ, His Word, and faith. (2 Cor. 10:5)

Beware, therefore, when you have become certain what the clear teaching of the Word of God of election is, then from that to draw all sorts of conclusions of reason. No, then much better, put your finger on your mouth, and do not want to know more about it than what God, in His Word, has revealed. Fear then the question, through which Satan once led our mother astray: "Yea, hath God said (that)?" (Gen. 3:1) Also, do not ask with Nicodemus, "How can such a thing happen?" (John 3:9)[3] For if you do that, you have already fallen away from God's Word.

Instead, speak humbly, with Samuel, to God: "Speak, Lord, for thy servant heareth." (1 Sam. 3:10) If you find that two doctrines are clearly and distinctly revealed in the Holy Scripture which appear to contradict each other, you must not attempt to fit the two together with reason, much less accept the one and reject the other, but then you must believe both from your heart and wait until eternal life, when God will then reveal to you how both doctrines harmonize most splendidly with each other.

Many have already thought and said, "In the Bible it says that there is only one God, and yet is also there that there are God the Father, God the Son, and God the Holy Ghost; that cannot be harmonized!" Some have therefore, following their reason, concluded: So only the Father can be the real God; others, against that, likewise following their reason, have accepted three Gods; and thus both have scandalously played away and lost the true God, and therewith their salvation. Oh, beware, therefore, dear reader, of such a will to harmonize! Now, as well, many want to solve and lay out for their reason the incomprehensible and unsearchable secrets which the doctrine of election contains, as they say: "Why the elect are elect is explained, in that God foresaw their behavior, that they namely accept the Gospel in faith, at every cross and under all assaults remain firm, and persevere in true faith until the end." Actually, many now say, to justify this rationalization, that many pure teachers of our Church have taught that the elect have been elected

---

[3] KJV: "How can these things be?"

in view of the foreseen faith;[4] if our present opponents only taught this, they would not declare our doctrine heretical, and much less would we declare them heretical, although we certainly hold the mode of teaching that God has elected in anticipation of foreseen faith to be a misunderstanding, which not only can be misused easily for false teaching, but really has been misused and still is misused that way.

Therefore, then, the Formula of Concord also warns expressly against this, to make inferences from God's foreknowledge and from that draw conclusions. Therefore beware, dear reader, of harmonizing the article of faith with your reason! Leave to God his secrets unsearched, and do not wonder that God knows more than you, and that he, in his secret determinations, does not let us poor, shortsighted people, yes, not even angels and archangels, see until the day of revelation of His glory.

Luther says in his House Postil: "The Bible and Scripture is not such a book that flows out of reason or human wisdom. Therefore, whoever undertakes to measure and calculate the Scripture, as if it fits together with reason, is going away from it. For all heretics, from the beginning to now, arose from their thinking that what they read in the Scripture, they would like to understand as reason teaches....St. Augustine complains that he initially went into the Scripture with free reason, and studied in it for nine years, and wanted to comprehend the Scripture with his reason. But the more he studied in it, the less he understood of it, until he finally discovered with his harm, that one must put reason's eyes out and say, "What the Scripture says, I leave unsearched by reason, but believe it with a simple heart." When one does that, Scripture becomes bright and clear, that formerly was dark. Thus says also St. Gregory, "The Holy Scripture is water in which an elephant swims and drowns; but a lamb goes through it as through a brook that is barely damp."

At another place, Luther writes, "If harmonizing should work, we would retain no article of faith."

Consider this further, though, dear reader: The present little writing has not been written so that one reads it through once quickly and then puts it away. From that, you would have little use. Instead, read it repeatedly and study it with prayer and pleading to God for the light of His Holy Ghost. For because the whole little book is taken from our Confession, you have in it an exceedingly rich treasure of teaching, which our dear Lutheran Church

---

[4]This teaching was called *intuitu fidei*—foreknowledge of faith. Some of the otherwise orthodox theologians of the late 16th and early 17th century taught this, as did a school of Reformed theologians called Amyraldians.

has left to us as a precious prize taken and carried away from from long and hard fighting for true safekeeping.

Should this little book perhaps also fall into the hands of a reader who is still not an actively faithful Christian, we advise him to read it either not at all, or at least not sooner than until he has become an actively believing Christian. For before that, what this little book contains is still no food for him. The most necessary question for him, much more, is: "What must I do to be saved?" and the one thing that is needful to him is then, that he first comes, on the way to true repentance to God, to true faith in Jesus Christ. For where the light of a living faith does not yet light up his heart, one can not do otherwise than to be bothered and angered by the doctrine of election, especially where it is not presented according to reason but rather according to God's Word.

Hence Luther writes in his golden Preface to the Epistle of St. Paul to the Romans:

Follow this Epistle in its order. Concern yourself first with Christ and the Gospel, that you may recognize your sin and His grace. After that, struggle with sin, as the 1st to the 8th chapters here have taught. After that, when you [namely in your experience] have come into the 8th chapter, under the Cross and suffering, that will teach you rightly about providence in the 9th to the 11th chapters, how comforting it is. For without suffering, cross and deadly need, one cannot deal with providence without harm and covert anger against God. Therefore Adam must previously be fully dead before he suffers this thing and drinks the strong wine. Therefore, take care that you do not drink wine when you are still a suckling. Every doctrine has its measure, time and age. (Walch XIV:125 ff.)

Hence, no one should buy and read this, our little writing, for our sake. We will therefore not send it to anyone, or let it be sent to anyone who does not desire it, or who we do not know wants it. For when one sends his writings to those who really do not desire them at all, that is nothing but sneaking around in corners; and when one entirely seeks to smuggle his writings into strange congregations, in order to stir up in them dispute and division, to sow distrust and suspicion, and especially to strengthen those, who desire to make trouble in their congregation, or who are under church discipline or actually excommunicated—that is even more scandalous, and a sure sign that such writers want to bring false goods, namely false doctrine, to the man.

Hear our dear Luther on this. After he, in his exposition of the 82nd Psalm, warned of *sneaks*[5] who grasp after an office that is not

---
[5]Emphasis in original.

theirs, he makes the following remark: "Here perhaps you say to me, 'why do you teach, then, the whole world in your books, since you are only preacher in Wittenberg?'" and answers now,

> I am a called preacher and want to teach those who are mine with writings. If now others have wanted my writings and have asked me for them, I have been obligated to do that, for I have nowhere pushed myself in, nor desired or asked anyone to read them, just as other pious pastors and preachers write more books, and neither prevent nor force anyone to read them, and with that, teach and run through the whole world, and do not sneak like the loose, uncalled rascals in offices that are not theirs without the knowledge or the wish of the pastors. (Walch V:1062-1063).

Now before we close this preface, the following should yet be noted: At the end of every answer, there are numbers in brackets [ ]. The first of these numbers is the page number of the Müller edition of the Book of Concord, which is also given in the jubilee edition, but on the edge. The second of these numbers, however, designates the paragraph number, which is however only given in the Müller edition. With the help of these numbers, every reader can quickly be persuaded that all answers are not our words, but are taken word for word from our Formula of Concord.[6]

God has given to our American Lutheran church, through the controversy over the doctrine of election the great task of fighting for one of the most secret-filled doctrines of His Word, which idle, irreverent, ambitious spirits, or negligent false Christians, are not capable or competent to evaluate, but only true, humble, enlightened Christians who care about their salvation and fear God's Word. This controversy over the doctrine of election is about the great, weighty questions: "Whom have those who come to faith, remain in the faith, and are saved have to thank for this? Can they thank themselves? Or can they thank themselves at least in part? Or have they only God's mercy and Christ's most holy merits to thank? Is God alone due the honor of our salvation? Or does it also have a cause in the person? Does a person have natural powers to cooperate to some extent in the work of his salvation, to decide himself for salvation, at least the word "Yes," however weakly? Or is every person by nature spiritually dead, and must God do everything through His grace?"

Yes, the present doctrinal controversy is about these great

---

[6] Instead of the Müller edition, which is in German and no longer in general circulation, the page and paragraph numbers in the brackets will be to Paul T. McCain and Edward A. Engelbrecht, ed., *Concordia: The Lutheran Confessions*, 2nd ed. (St. Louis: Concordia Publishing House, 2006); this is a current English edition readily available, revising the 1921 Dau-Bente edition ("Triglotta").

truths, of the doctrine of salvation by grace alone, for the sake of Christ alone, through faith granted by God alone, not about theological niceties, but about the most important points of practical Christianity. May God then have mercy on our American Lutheran Zion, and help that no rightly formed soul goes into error in this fight for the truth, but that all true children of God within our church gather under the good old banner of our confession regarding this doctrine, and thus become a light for many in this midnight hour of our latest dark times.

May God do that, for the sake of Jesus Christ, the savior of all sinners and eternal King of truth. Amen.

C.F.W.W.

The Doctrine of Election
in Question and Answer

1. What is election in short words?
God's predestination to salvation. [498,4]

2. What distinction is to be noted diligently in the doctrine of election right at the start?
At the start, the distinction between foreknowledge and eternal election (predestination) is to be noted. [498,2]

3. What is the foreknowledge of God?
The foreknowledge of God is that God sees everything in advance and knows it before it happens. [498,3]

4. Does the foreknowledge of God extend over all creatures?
Yes; the foreknowledge of God extends over all creatures, over the pious and the evil alike. He knows everything in advance and knows, what is or will be, what happens or will happen, be it good or bad, because all things, be they past or future, are unconcealed and present before God. As it is written in Matt. 10:29: "Does one not buy two sparrows for a penny? Yet of them, not one falls to the earth without your Father."[7] And Ps. 139:16: "Thy eyes saw me, when I was yet unfinished, and all days that yet should be were written in thy book , when of them none were yet there." Likewise

---

[7] To convey best Walther's understanding of the Scripture passages he quotes, all Bible passages are translated from his German, unless otherwise noted.

Is. 37:28: I know thy going out and going in, and thy rage against me." [702,4]

5. Does the eternal election of God, just like the foreknowledge, extend over all people, good and bad?
No. The eternal election of God, that is, God's predestination to salvation does not extend to the pious and the wicked, but solely to the children of God. [602-603, 5]

6. To what kind of children of God does, then, the eternal election of God extend?
Only to those children of God who were elected and preordained to eternal life, before the foundation of the world was laid. [603,5]

7. With what do you prove from Scripture that eternal election is not to everyone, but extends only to the children of God who have been preordained to eternal life?
Paul says, Eph. 1:4-5: "He has elected us in Christ Jesus and preordained us to be His children." [603,6]

8. Does God's foreknowledge not only not see evil in advance, but is it also a cause of evil?
The foreknowledge of God sees and knows evil in advance as well, but not in such a way that it would be God's gracious will that it happen; rather, what the perverted evil will of the devil and of people will undertake and want to do, God sees and knows in advance, and maintains His foreknowledge even in the wicked doings or works of their order, so that God gives the evil that He does not want, His appointed goal and measure, how far it should go, how long it should last, and when and how He will hinder or punish it; all of which God, the Lord, thus rules, that it may provide His name with honor and to His elect, well being, and the Godless thereby must be put to shame. [603,6]

9. Is God's foreknowledge, then, the cause of evil, which it sees and knows in advance?
No. The beginning and cause of evil is not God's foreknowledge (for God does not make or work evil, nor does He help or further it), but the devil's and people's evil and perverted will, as is written, "Israel, thou bringest thyself into misfortune; but thy salvation is with me alone." (Hos. 13:9)[8] Likewise, "Thou art not a God whom

---

[8] Walther is quoting from Luther's Bible. See also KJV: "O Israel, thou hast destroyed thyself; but in me is thine help." *Concordia* quotes from the ESV: "He destroys you, O Israel, for you are against me, against your helper." [603,7] The Formula of Concord's, and Walther's, point is clearer in the older translations.

Godless conduct pleases." Ps. 5:5.[9]

10. Does the election of God only see and know the salvation of the elect in advance, or it it also a cause of their salvation and of everything that pertains to the attainment of the same?

The eternal election of God not only sees and knows in advance the salvation of the elect, but is also, by the gracious will and favor of God in Christ Jesus *a cause, that shapes, works, helps and furthers our salvation and all that pertains to it.* [603-604,8]

11. Is it then so important that the eternal election of God is a cause of our salvation and that it makes, works, helps and furthers everything that pertains to it?

Yes, certainly! For on that, our salvation is so grounded, that "the gates of hell should not prevail against it." (Matt. 16:18) [604,8]

12. From what do you prove that the salvation of the elect is so unshakeably firmly founded on the eternal election?

From that it is written, "No one will rip[10] my sheep out of My hand." (John 10:28) And again: "And so many became believers as were preordained to eternal life." (Acts 13:48). [604,8]

13. Is it right, if one regards eternal election as being only in the secret, unsearchable counsel of God?

No. The same eternal election or predestination of God to eternal life is also not only in the secret, unsearchable counsel of God, as if it consisted of nothing more than that God decreed in advance, who and how many are saved, who and how many would be damned, or that He only made a sort of roll call: "This one should be saved, this one should be damned; this one will persevere, that one will not persevere." [604,9]

14. Why should one not regard election as if it contained nothing more than that God decreed in advance, who and how many should be saved, who and how many should be damned?

This is why: For from that many take and put together strange, dangerous and harmful thoughts, to cause and strengthen either security and unrepentance, or timidity and despair, that they fall into accursed thought and say, "Because God has foreseen His elect, before the foundation of the world was laid (Eph. 1:4), and God's

---

[9] Again, this is a translation of Walther, quoting Luther's Bible. KJV: "thou hatest all workers of iniquity." ESV: "You are not a God who delights in wickedness."

[10] ESV: "snatch"

foreknowledge does not fail, nor can be hindered or changed by anyone (Is. 14:27; Rom. 9:19), if I am then predestined to salvation, nothing can harm me in that, even if I, unrepentantly, commit all sorts of sin and scandal, despise Word and Sacrament, nor concern myself with repentance, faith, prayer or the holiness of God, I will and must be saved, for God's foreknowledge must happen; but if I am not elect, then it does not help, even if I hold to the word, do penance, believe, etc., for I cannot hinder or change God's foreknowledge." [604,10]

15. Do, then, even true Christians fall into such harmful thoughts, when they regard eternal election according to reason?

Yes. Such thoughts also fall into truly God-blessed souls, even when they, by God's grace, have repentance, faith and good intentions, when they think: "But if you are not predestined from eternity to salvation, then it's all a waste," and especially when they look at their weakness and at the example of those who did not persevere, but fell away again. [604,11; 498,9]

16. What is a clear, certain reason, which cannot fail, which one can set up against these false delusions and thoughts about election?

It is this: Because all Scripture was given by God not for security and unrepentance, but should serve for admonition, correction and betterment, 2 Tim. 3:16; likewise because everything is therefore prescribed for us in God's Word, not that we should be driven thereby into despair, but that we through patience and comfort of the Scripture have hope. Rom. 15:4: thus it is without any doubt in no way that through the healthy understanding or right use of the doctrine of the eternal foreknowledge of God either unrepentance or despair should be caused or reinforced. [604,12]

17. How does the holy Scripture present this doctrine?

Not otherwise than thus, that it points us to the Word, Eph. 1:13; 1 Cor.1:7, admonishes us to repentance, 2 Tim. 3:16, holds us to Godliness, Eph. 1; John 15:3, strengthens faith, and makes our salvation more certain. Eph. 1; John 10:27 ff; 2 Thess. 2:13 ff. [604,12]

18. May one then hold the doctrine of election to be useless or even harmful?

No. One cannot and should not the teaching of this article, when it is taught from and according to the example of the divine Word, to be useless or unnecessarily, much less to be annoying or harmful, because the Holy Scripture does not recall this article only at one place, but deals with and promotes it thoroughly at many places. [602,2]

19. But should one not rather remain silent about the doctrine of election because of its misuse and misunderstanding?

Far from it! One must not drop or reject the teaching of the divine Word because of misuse or misunderstanding, but precisely for that reason, to drive off all misuse and misunderstanding, the right understanding must be explained on the basis of the Scripture. [602,2]

20. What should be our custom, when one wants to think or speak about eternal election or from the predestination and preordaining of the cihldren of God to eternal life rightly and fruitfully?

One should become accustomed, that one does not speculate about the bare, secret, hidden, unsearchable foreknowledge of God, but as the counsel, precept and prescription of God in Christ Jesus, who is the true Book of Life, is *revealed* to us in the Word;[11] namely that the whole teaching of the precept, counsel, will and order of God, touching our redemption, calling, justification and salvation is collected together; as *Paul* handles this article and explains it in Rom. 8:29 ff.; Eph. 1:4 ff, as Christ also did in a parable (Matt. 22:1 ff). [604-605, 13-14]

21. What has God first ordered in His plan and counsel, as the same has been revealed to us through the Word in Christ?

That the human race is truly redeemed and reconciled with God through Christ, who has earned for us with His innocent obedience, suffering and death righteousness valid before God, and eternal life. [605,15]

22. What has God further in His plan and counsel ordered, how the same is revealed to us in Christ through the Word?

That He wants to justify all those, who accept Christ in true repentance through a right faith, and accept them into grace, adoption as children, and inheritance of eternal life.

That He also wants to sanctify those thus justified, in love, as St. Paul says in Eph. 1:4.

That He also wants to protect them in their great weakness against devil, world and flesh, and rule and lead them on His ways, set them upright when they stumble, comfort them in Cross and assaults, and preserve them.

---

[11] All emphasis in italics in this book is in the original; at the one place where the translator has added emphasis, it was done by capitalizing the word stressed.

That He also wants to strengthen and increase in them the good work that He has begun, and preserve them to the end, where they hold themselves to God's Word, pray diligently, remain in God's goodness, and use the received gifts faithfully.

23. What has God finally ordained in His plan and counsel, how the same is revealed to us in Christ through the Word?

That He finally wants to make the same whom He has elected, called and justified also eternally saved and made glorious in eternal life as well. [605,15-22]

24. Then has God in this his counsel, plan and preordaining prepared only in general the salvation of His own?

No. God has in this His counsel, plan and preordaining, covered all and every person of the elect, who should be saved through Christ in grace, elected them to salvation, also *preordained* that he, in the way just mentioned, through His grace, gifts and work *wishes to bring, help, advance, strengthen and preserve them.*

25. Does all this really belong, then, to the doctrine of election?

Yes. All this is comprehended according to the Scripture in the doctrine of the eternal election of God to adoption and eternal salvation, and should be understood and never excluded or dropped, when one speaks of the plan, foreknowledge, election and predestination of God to salvation. [605,23-24]

26. Can the doctrine of election cause security or despair, when one thus presents it, when one namely first lays the foundation of the general redemption of Christ and on this shows the way, how God brings the elect to salvation?

No; when the thoughts of this article are put together thus according to the Scripture, one can guide himself simply through God's grace. [605,24]

27. What now belongs to further explanation and wholesome use of the doctrine of the predestination of God to salvation?

This: how one can know, from what and in what one can recognize, who the elect are, who can and should take this doctrine to their comfort. [605,25]

28. Why does it belong to the wholesome use of this doctrine, that one knows who the elect are?

Because only the elect are saved. [605,25]

29. According to what should one not judge, when one wants to know, who the elect are?

From these we should not judge: according to our reason, also not according to the Law, or from some outward appearance; we should also not undertake to find the secret, hidden abyss of divine foreknowledge. [605,26]

30. To what should we give much more attention, when we want to recognize who the elect are, who can and should accept this doctrine to their comfort?

We should pay attention to the revealed will of God, for "he has revealed to us and let us know the secret of His will, and has brought the same out through Jesus, that it is preached." Eph. 1:9 ff, 2 Tim. 1:9, ff. [605,26]

31. But how is the secret of the will of God revealed to us?

That is revealed to us as St. Paul says in Rom. 8:29 ff.: Whom God foreknew, elected and predestined, He also *called.*" [606,27]

32. How does this call happen?

God does not call without means, but through the Word, as he has "commanded to preach repentance and forgiveness of sins." (Luke 24:47). Likewise, St. Paul witnesses, as he wrote: "We are ambassadors in Christ's stead, and God admonishes through us: Let yourselves be reconciled with God." (2 Cor. 5:20) And the guests whom the King wants to have at the wedding of His Son, He calls through His sent servants (Matt. 22:2 ff), some in the first, some in the second, third, sixth, ninth, even in the eleventh hour. (Matt.20:3 ff) [606,27]

33. What must we therefore, when we want to see our eternal election to salvation in a useful way, hold hard and fast?

This: that, like the preaching of repentance, so also the universal promise of the Gospel, that is, it extends to all people. Luke 24:47. Therefore Christ has commanded to preach in His name "repentance and forgiveness of sins to all people." (Luke 24:47) For "God has loved the world and given to the same His son" (John 3:16) John 1:29; 6:51; 1 John 5:6; 2:2. Matt. 11:28. Rom. 11:32; 3:22; John 6:40. Thus it is commanded of Christ, that in general also this promise of the Gospel should be presented to all to whom repentance is preached. Luke 24:47; Mark 16:15. [606,28]

34. Is then the call of God through the Word always meant seriously?

Yes. Such a call of God, which occurs through the preaching of the Word, we should not treat as a sham, but know that through it God reveals His will, that He wants to work through His Word in those whom He calls in this way, that they maybe enlightened, converted, and saved. For the Word, through which we are called, is an office of the Spirit, that the Spirit gives, or through which the Spirit is given (2 Cor. 3:8), and a power of God to save. (Rom. 1:16) And because the Holy Ghost wants to be powerful through the Word, strengthen, and give power and capability, it is thus God's will that we accept the Word, and should believe and follow the same. [606,29]

35. How therefore are those who belong to the elect described in the Scripture, so that everyone can know, if he belongs to them?

Hence the elect are described thus (John 10:27 ff), "My sheep hear my voice, and I know them, and they follow me, and I give them eternal life." And Eph:1:11-13, "Who according to the decree are preordained to a part of the inheritance," who hear the Gospel, believe in Christ, pray and give thanks, are sanctified in love, have hope, patience and comfort in the Cross (Rom. 8:25); and although all this is very weak in them, they nonetheless have hunger and thirst after righteousness. (Matt. 5:6) Thus the Spirit of God gives the elect, "Witness that they are children of God, and when they do not know what they should pray as they ought, He represents them with unspeakable sighs." (Rom. 8:16,26) [607,31]

36. Must we not doubt, though, whether we are elect, when we remember that so many who were called and who came to faith, did not persevere to the end?

In no way. The Holy Scripture also shows that God, who has called us, is so faithful, when He has begun the good work in us, also wants to maintain and complete it to the end, when we do not ourselves turn away from him, but retain that which has been begun until the end. For that, He has promised His grace. 1 Cor. 1:9; Phil. 1:6; 1 Pet. 5:10; 2 Pet. 3:9; Heb.3. [607,32]

37. What should we then do, since God's will is so clearly revealed to us in the Word?

We should concern ourselves with this revealed will of God, follow it, and busy ourselves with it, because the Holy Ghost, through the Word, through which He calls us, adds thereto grace, power and capacity, and not probe the hidden foreknowledge of God; as is written in Luke 13:24, where someone asks, "Lord, meanest thou that few are saved?" and Christ answers, "Struggle, that you may go through the narrow gate." [607,33]

38. But when will a person first learn to understand, how comforting the doctrine of election is?

Luther speaks of this in his preface to St. Paul's Epistle to the Romans: "Follow the Epistle to the Romans in its order. Concern yourself first with Christ and His Gospel, that you recognize your sin and His grace, after that that struggle with sin, as Paul teaches from the 1st into the 8th chapter. After that, when you, in the 8th chapter, come to assaults under cross and suffering, that will teach you how comforting predestination is, in the 9th, 10th, and 11th chapters," etc.. Whoever concerns himself in that way with the revealed will of God, and goes according to the order which St. Paul kept in the Epistle to the Romans, which first points to repentance, to recognition of sins, to faith in Christ, and to Godly obedience, before he speaks of the secret of eternal election, for him such a teaching is useful and comforting. [607,33; 499,11]

39. But is it not written, "Many are called but few are chosen"? How then can the call be a certain sign through which God reveals the secret of His will for us?

Yes; that many are called and few chosen, does not come with a meaning as if God said, "Outwardly, through the Word, I do call you all, to whom I give My Word, to My Kingdom, but in my heart, I do not mean all, but just some few; for it is My will that the greater part of those whom I call through the Word should not be enlightened nor converted, but be and remain damned, even if I, through the Word, declare otherwise in the call. [607,34]

40. Why would it be against God to assume, that God, to be sure, outwardly calls to salvation, but means it otherwise in His heart?

This is why: Because this would mean, God forms contradicting wills; that is, with such a construct it would be taught that God, who is after all the eternal Truth, is against Himself, while God punishes in people such wickedness, that one declares one thing and thinks and intends something different in one's heart. Ps. 5:10; 12:3 ff. [607,35]

41. What necessary foundation of our faith would be overturned if we could not believe that God reveals the secret of His will toward us through the call?

Through that, the necessary, comforting foundation would be totally uncertain and made nothing, that we are daily reminded and admonished that we should learn and determine what His will toward us and what He grants and promises is solely from God's Word, through which He deals with us and calls us, so that we should believe that certainly and not doubt it. [607,36]

42. What has Christ therefore ordained, which which every single Christian can draw also to himself in particular the general promise of the Gospel?

Christ therefore does not let the promise of the Gospel be presented only in general, but seals the same also through the Sacraments, which He has added as a seal of the promise, and confirms it thereby also to every single believer in particular. [607,37]

43. Do we not also retain for exactly that reason private absolution, with which every individual thereby would become certain of the will of God for him?

Yes. Exactly for that reason we retain also, as the Augsburg Confession says in article 11, private confession, and teach that it is God's commandment that we should believe such absolution and hold it as certain that we truly, when we believe the word of absolution, are reconciled to God, as if we had heard a voice from heaven, as the Apology explains this article. This comfort is completely taken away from us when we do not determine about God's will toward us from the call which happens through the Word and through the Sacraments. [608,38]

44. Would not also the doctrine of the power of the Word be overthrown if we could not recognize God's gracious will toward us from our call through the Word?

Certainly; through that, also the foundation that the Holy Ghost wants to be certainly present in the preached, heard and read Word, and through that be powerful and work would be overthrown and taken away. [608,39]

45. Can then, because many are called and few are chosen, also those be elect who ignore the Word by which they are called?

No. It does not in any way mean that namely those can be the elect, even if they despise the Word of God, push it away from themselves, abuse it and persecute it (Matt. 22:6; Acts 13:46), or, when they hear it, harden their hearts (Heb. 4:2,7) strive against the Holy Ghost (Acts 7:51), persist without repenting in sins (Luke 14:18), do not truly believe in Christ (Mark 16:16), maintain only an outward appearance (Matt. 7:22; 22:12), or seek other ways to justification and salvation outside of Christ (Rom. 9:31). [608,39]

46. For what has God at once, in His eternal counsel, preordained those who are elect to salvation?

In order that the Holy Ghost may, through the Word, call, enlighten and convert the elect, and that He may make all who through true faith accept Jesus righteous and saved. [608,40]

47. But what has God, at the same time, in His counsel, also concluded about those who do not follow the call?
This—that He will harden, reject and damn them when they push the Word away from themselves and work against the Holy Ghost, who wants to be powerful and work in them through the Word. [608,40]

48. Then why are many called and few chosen?
Because few accept the Word and follow it, the great crowd ignores the Word and does not want to come to the wedding. [608,40-41]

49. So what is not the cause of such ignoring of the Word?
God's predestination is not the reason for such ignoring of the Word, but rather the perverted human will, which pushes away from itself or perverts the means and tools of the Holy Ghost, as God presents them to it, and works against the Holy Ghost, who wants to be powerful through the Word and works. As Christ says, "How often have I wanted to gather thee, and thou wouldst not." Matt. 23:37 [608,41]

50. What is also not the cause that to be sure many receive the Word with joy, but thereafter fall away? (Luke 8:13)
The cause is not that God did not want to give them in whom He had begun the good work the grace to perseverance; for that is against St. Paul in Phil. 1:6; but the cause is, because they willfully turned away again from the Holy Ghost, grieve and embitter the Holy Spirit, go back into the filth of the world, and redecorate the inn of their heart for the devil, with whom the last one is worse than the first. (2 Peter 2:10,20; Eph. 4:30; Heb. 10:26; Luke 11:25 [608,42]

51. Is then the doctrine of election useless, or even harmful, when it is so regarded as it is revealed in God's Word, and when we stay with it and hold to it?
No. That way, it is really a useful, wholesome, comforting doctrine. [608,43]

52. What principal article of the Christian faith does the doctrine of election confirm, when it is regarded and presented according to God's Word?

It confirms forcefully the article that we, without all our works and merits, purely by grace, solely for the sake of Christ, are justified and saved. [608,43]

53. How, then, does the true doctrine of election confirm the doctrine of justification (solely by grace for the sake of Christ) so forcefully?

Because we, according to the doctrine of election, were elected to salvation, yes, before the foundation of the world was laid, since we could have done no good, by God's plan, out of grace in Christ. (Rom. 9:11; 2 Tim. 1:9[12] [608-609,43]

54. Is, then, the true doctrine of election not only in general comforting, but also giving every single Christian individually comfort personally?

Yes. This doctrine also gives the beautiful, splendid comfort, that God made every single Christian's conversion, justification and salvation such a high concern, and meant it so honestly, that He, before the foundation of the earth was laid, took counsel and *in His plan ordained* how He *wanted to bring me to that and keep me in it.* [609,45]

55. Does the true doctrine of election then give Christians such a beautiful, splendid comfort when they think about it, that they could so easily lose their salvation through the weakness and wickedness of their flesh, or through the trickery and force of the devil and the world?

Yes. The true doctrine of election also gives the beautiful, splendid comfort, that God wanted so much and so certainly to realize *my* salvation, because it could have been so easily lost out of our hands through weakness and wickedness of our flesh, or ripped out by the trickery and force of the devil and the world, that He *ordained* it in His eternal *plan, which cannot fail or be overthrown*, and put it in the almighty hand of our Savior, Jesus Christ, out of which no one can rip us, to preserve it. John 10:28; hence also Paul says (Rom. 8:28,39): "Because we are called according to the plan of God, who will then sever us from the love of God in Christ?" '[609, 46-47]

56. Does the true doctrine of also give us a deep comfort under cross and assault?

Yes. This doctrine also gives splendid comfort also under cross and assault, namely, that God in His counsel before all time con-

---

[12] See also Eph. 1:4.

ceived the world and decided that He would stand by us in all trouble, grant us patience, give us comfort, work hope in us, and make such an outcome that we could be saved; also, as Paul handles this so comfortingly in Rom. 8:28,29,35,38 and 39, that God "in His plan before time, ordered the world," through which cross and suffering He wished to make every single one of His elect just like an image of His Son and that every single one's cross *should and must serve him for the best*, because they are called according to His plan; from which Paul concluded as certain and undoubted that "neither trouble nor fear, neither death nor life," etc., "can sever us from the love of God in Christ Jesus." [609, 48-49]

57. Does the true doctrine of election also give the comfort that the Church cannot perish despite the persecution of tyrants and despite the seductions of the heretics?
Yes. This article also gives a splendid witness that the Church of God will be and remain against all gates of hell. [609,50]

58. Does the true doctrine of election also give comfort against the outrage that things go so badly for the true Church and so well for the false one in this world?
Yes, for it also teaches which is the true Church of God, that we are not outraged at the great respect accorded the false Church. Rom. 9:24-25 [609,50]

59. Does the true doctrine of election contain not only comfort but also admonitions and warnings?
Yes. Many powerful admonitions and warnings are to be taken from this article. For example, Luke 7:30: "They despise God's counsel against themselves." Luke 14:24: "I say to you, that none of those men will taste my banquet." Also, Matt. 20:16: "Many are called, but few are chosen." Also, Luke 8:8: "He who has ears to hear, let him hear." Luke 8:18: "See to it how you hear." [609,51]

60. How can the doctrine of this article be used after this?
Usefully, comfortingly, and blessedly. [609,51]

61. What kind of distinction must be observed with regard to election in teaching the same?
The distinction must be maintained with special diligence between that which is expressly revealed in God's Word about this and that which is not revealed. [609,52]

62. Has God not revealed to us everything concerning election?

No; for about this, as was said before, as was revealed in Christ, God has remained silent and concealed much about this secret, and kept it to His wisdom and knowledge alone. [610,52]

63. Should we also seek to find out with our reason the secrets of election that are not revealed in God's Word?

No. We should not attempt to find them out, nor follow, nor reach conclusions with, our thoughts, nor ponder, but hold to the revealed Word. [610,52]

64. Why is the reminder that we should not reach conclusions or ponder, so highly necessary?

Because our excessive curiousity always has more desire to concern itself with that which God has reserved to His wisdom, than with that which God has revealed about it in His Word, because we cannot harmonize it, which we are also not commanded to do. [610,53]

65. But is it not certain that God has already foreseen from eternity and still knows what will certainly happen?

Yes. Of that there is no doubt, that God has foreseen and still knows very well and most certainly who, if called, will believe or not believe; also, which of the converted will persevere, which will not persevere; which after falling away will return, which will fall into hardening. So the number, how many of those will be on each side, is without doubt known to God. [610,54]

66. May we, however, draw all kinds of conclusions from the fact that God has already foreseen and knows everything?

No, for, because God has reserved such secrets to His wisdom and revealed nothing of them in the Word, much less ordered us to discover through our thoughts, but has ernestly refrained from doing so (Rom. 11:33), we should not pursue, nor draw conclusions from, nor ponder, such thoughts, but hold to His revealed Word, to which He directs us. [610,55]

67. But does not God also know the time and hour of the calling and conversion of every person, and has He not Himself determined, when He will call and convert him?

Yes. God knows without any doubt, and has determined for

---

[13] The clause in parentheses is from Chemnitz's revised Latin translation.

everyone the time of his calling and conversion, (and when, if he has fallen, He will set him upright again.)[13] [610,56]

68. So should preachers with their preaching and hearers with their hearing wait on the hour determined by God?

Far from it! Instead, because such is not revealed to us, we have the command that we always hold onto the Word; God will order the time and hour. Acts 1:7. [610,56]

69. Do we not also see that God, in the distribution of His grace, shows Himself quite differently as to whole countries and single people, although the same may be in the same guilt?

Certainly, yes. We see that God gives His Word at one place, at another does not give it; takes it away from one place, at another, lets it remain; likewise, one will be hardened, blinded, and given over into a perverted mind, another, who may well be in the same guilt, is once more converted, etc.. [610,57]

70. How should we, then, judge from this secret, that God deals so differently with people, and apply it to our salvation?

In this and similar questions, Paul sets for us a certain goal, how far we should go, namely, that we should recognize *God's judgment* by one part. For those are well-earned punishments of sins when God punishes a country or a people for its despising of His Word in such a way that it also extends to those who follow, as can be seen with the Jews;[14] through which God shows His own in some countries and people what we would all certainly have earned and of what we would have been worthy, because we behave ourselves evilly with regard to God's Word and often greatly distress the Holy Ghost. This He does so that we may live in the fear of God and recognize and praise *God's goodness* to and with us, to whom He gives and leaves His Word, whom he does not harden and reject. [610,58-59]

71. Why do we have to recognize God's just judgment on those from whom He takes His Word and who remain hardened and blinded?

This is why: 1. For while our nature, corrupted by sin, is guilty and worthy of God's wrath and damnation, God does not owe us Word, Spirit or grace; and 2. if He gives these things out of grace, we often push them away from ourselves and make ourselves unworthy of eternal life. Acts 13:46. [610,60]

---

[14] See Exodus 20:5, and Matt. 27:25. This should not be taken to justify what happened in Germany, 1933-45, or later at various times in the Soviet Union.—Tr.

72. Then why does God let us, who have God's grace and Word, see His just, well-deserved judgment on some lands, nations and people?

So that we, when held up next to and compared to them, learn that much more diligently to recognize and praise God's pure grace at the vessels of mercy. For it does not happen unfairly to them who are punished and receive the wages of their sins. To the others, however, where God gives and preserves His Word and the people are thereby enlightened, converted and preserved, God awards His pure grace and mercy without their merit. [610-611,60-61]

73. So do we stay on the right path, when we, without pondering and drawing conclusions about God's justice to them who experience God's judgment, recognize His pure, unearned grace in them to whom God gives His Word and enlightens and preserves them?

Yes, when we go that far in this article, we remain on the right path, as is written in Hosea 13:9: "Israel, that you *become corrupt*, the *guilt* is *thine*; that you are *helped*, that is *purely my grace*."[15] [611,62]

74. So is it right, if one wants, in this article of election, to harmonize, explore and analyze everything?

No. Whatever in this dispute runs too high and out of these bounds, we should, with Paul, put our finger on our mouth, consider, and say, "Who art thou, man, that thou shouldst argue with God?"[16] [611,63]

75. Does not also the high Apostle Paul himself testify that we neither can nor should harmonize, explore and analyze everything?

Yes, the high Apostle Paul, since he argues much about this article and the revealed Word of God, as soon as he comes to the point where he shows what God has reserved to His hidden wisdom, suppresses it and cuts it off with the following words: "Oh, what a depth of the richness, both of the wisdom and of the knowledge of God! How very incomprehensible are His judgments and unsearchable His ways!" namely what is outside and above that which He has revealed to us in His Word. [611,64]

76. Do we regard then the eternal election of God rightly, when we seek to find out the secret counsel of God?

---

[15] Walther is paraphrasing here; he has previously quoted the verse verbatim.—Tr.
[16] Rom. 9:20.

No. The eternal election of God should be observed in Christ and not outside of or without Christ. [611,65]

77. How do you prove that the eternal election of God should be observed in Christ and not outside of or without Christ?

With this: the holy Apostle Paul testifies, "we were elected before the foundation of the world was laid;" as is written, "He has loved us in the Beloved." Eph. 1:4 ff. [611,65]

78. But through what does such election from heaven become apparent to us?

Through the preached Word; for the Father says, "This is my beloved Son, in whom I am well pleased; you should hear Him." (Matt. 17:5) And Christ says, "Come here to me, all you who are burdened, I will refresh you." (Matt. 11:28) And of the Holy Ghost, Christ says, "He will glorify Me and remind you of everything that I have said to you." (John 16:14) [611,65]

79. To whom then does the whole Holy Trinity, God the Father, Son and Holy Ghost, direct all people, in that they should seek the Father's eternal election?

To Christ, as to the book of life. [611,66]

80. How do you prove that the whole Trinity directs all people to Christ, in whom they should seek the Father's eternal election?

With three reasons: for 1. that has been decided from eternity by the *Father*; whom He wants to save, He wants to save through Christ. As Christ Himself says, "No one comes to the Father but by Me." (John 14:6) And again, "I am the Gate; if anyone goes in through me, he will be saved." (John 10:9)

Christ, however, as the only-begotten *Son* of God, who is in the bosom of the Father, has proclaimed to us the will of the Father, and thus also our eternal election to eternal life, namely where He says, "That is the will of Him who has sent me, that whoever sees the Son and believes in Him has eternal life." (John 6:40) And again, "God so loved the world," etc. (John 3:16). The Father wants that all people hear this preaching and should come to Christ, who will not drive them away, as is written, "Whoever comes to me, I will not push him away." (John 6:37)

And so that we may come to Christ, the *Holy Ghost* works true faith through the hearing of the Word, as the Apostle testifies, where he says, "So now faith comes from hearing God's Word," (Rom. 10:17), when the same is clearly and purely preached. [611,66-69]

81. So should a person who wants to be saved, exert and plague himself with thoughts of the secret counsel of God, if he, too, is elected and predestined to eternal life, with which Satan takes care to assault pious hearts and lead them into error?

By no means; instead they should hear Christ, who is the book of life and of the eternal election of God to eternal life for all children of God. He testifies to all people without distinction that God wills that "all people come to Him" who are burdened and laden, that they be refreshed and saved. (Matt. 11:28) [611-612,70]

82. What should therefore all who want to be saved do, according to this teaching of Christ, instead of plaguing themselves about God's secret counsel?

They should distance themselves from their sins, repent, believe His promise, and rely entirely on Him; and because we are not capable of that by our own powers, the Holy Ghost wants to work the same, namely repentance and faith, through the Word and through the Sacraments. And that we may complete that, persevere in it, and remain constant, we should call on God for His grace, which He has granted to us in holy Baptism, and not doubt, He will communicate the same to us according to His promise, as He promised in Luke 11:11 ff., "Wherever a son among you asks his father for bread,"[17] etc.. [612,71-72]

83. Then may believers, who can and should accept the doctrine of election for their comfort, be idle or even set themselves against the working of the Spirit of God?

No. After the elect have become believers, the Holy Ghost lives in them as in His temple (1 Cor. 3:16), and is not idle, but moves the children of God to obedience to the commandments of God; in the same way, believers should not be idle, much less set themselves against the working of the Spirit of God, but practice all Christian virtues, in all godliness, modesty, moderation, patience, brotherly love, and give all diligence that they "make their calling and election firm."[18] [612,73]

84. Why should believers, who can and should accept the doctrine of election to their comfort, not be idle, but practice all Christian virtues?

That they may doubt that much less, the more they find the

---

[17] Walther is, again quoting from Luther's translation, which uses the Received Text; some texts omit a phrase here and have only "asks his father for a fish," which is, in the Received Text, the phrase that follows. —Tr.

[18] 2 Peter 1:10.

power and strength of the Spirit in themselves. For the Spirit of God gives the elect witness, that they are children of God. (Rom. 8:16) [612,73]

85. But must not believers doubt their election and salvation when they do not feel the power of the Spirit?
Far from it! Even if they may come under such a heavy assault that they think they do not feel the power of the indwelling Spirit any more, and say with David (Ps. 31:22)[19] "I said in my despair,[20] I am put away from Thine eyes," then again they should say with David to that (regardless of what they find in themselves), as then follows immediately, "However, Thou heardest the voice of my pleading when I cried to Thee." [719,74]

86. But must we not doubt on our election and salvation because we can fall?
No. because our election to eternal life is not *founded* on our piety or virtue, but *solely* on Christ's merit and the gracious will of His Father, who cannot deny Himself, because He is unchangeable in His will and ways. Therefore, when His children step out of obedience and stumble, He lets them be called back to repentance through the Word, and the Holy Ghost thereby be powerful in them to conversion, and, when they in true repentance return to Him, He will always show the old fatherly love to all those who fear His Word and return to them in their hearts, as is written in Jer. 3:1. [612,75]

87. But must we perhaps doubt our election and salvation, because it is written, "No one can come to me unless the Father draw him"?
By no means: that it is said, no one comes to Christ unless the Father draw him (John 6:44) is right and true. But the Father does not want to do that without means, but has for that purpose ordained His Word and Sacrament as orderly means and tools, and it is neither the Father's nor the Son's will that a person should despise or not hear the preaching of His Word and wait for the drawing by the Father without Word and Sacrament. For the Father certainly draws with the power of His Holy Ghost, but according to His regular order, through the hearing of His holy, divine Word, as with a net, through which the elect are torn out of the grasp of the devil, on which every poor sinner should rely, hear the same diligently, and should not doubt the drawing of the Father. For the Holy Ghost wants to be with the Word and work through it with

---

[19] Walther erroneously gives verse number 23.
[20] German "Zagen"; KJV says "haste"; ESV says "alarm"—neither corresponds to the German.

His power; and that *is* the drawing of the Father. [613,76-77]

88. May one from that, that not all come to faith who have heard God's Word, draw the conclusion that God has not granted them salvation?

Not at all; for that not all those who have heard God's Word believe, and therefore so many are that much more deeply damned, the cause of that is not that God did not grant them salvation, but they are themselves at fault, who heard the Word in such a way, not to learn, but just to despise, abuse and disgrace it, and that they have striven against the Holy Ghost, who wanted to work in them, as was an attitude at the time of Christ with the Pharisees and their followers. [613,78]

89. Has God made "the vessels of wrath" and "of dishonor" of which Paul writes?

No. The apostle distinguishes with particular diligence the work of God, who only makes vessels of honor, and the work of the devil and of the person, who makes himself, under the influence of the devil and not of God, into a vessel of dishonor. For it is written in Rom. 9:22 ff.:

"God has borne the vessels of wrath with great patience, those that are fitted to damnation, so that He might make known the richness of His glory on the vessels of mercy, that He has prepared for salvation." Since then the apostle says clearly, God has borne the vessels of wrath with great patience, and does not say He has made them vessels of wrath; for if it were His will, He would not have needed any great patience. That they are, however, prepared for damnation is the fault of the devil and people themselves, and not of God. [613,79-80]

90. From where is then all preparation to damnation?

All preparation for damnation is from the devil and people, through sin, and absolutely not from God, who does not desire that a person be damned; how then could He Himself then prepare a person for damnation? [613,81]

91. So how do you prove that God is not the cause of the damnation of anyone?

As God is not a cause of sin, then He is also no cause of punishment, damnation; but the only cause of damnation is sin, for "the wage of sin is death." (Rom. 6:23) And as God does not want sin, and has no pleasure in sin, so "he also does not desire the death of a sinner." (Ezek. 33:11), and also has no pleasure in their damnation; for "he does not want that someone is lost, but that everyone turns to repentance." (2 Peter 3:9), as is written in Ezek. 18:23; 33:11: "I have no pleasure in the death of the dying. As truly as I live, I do not want the death of a sinner, but that he repent and live." [613,81]

92. May one conclude that since God Himself prepares the vessels of mercy, He Himself also prepares the vessels of dishonor?

No. St. Paul testifies with clear words that by God's power and working, vessels of dishonor may become vessels of honor, for he writes thus in 2 Tim. 2:21: "If now someone purifies himself from such people, he will be a sanctified vessel, prepared for honor to be useful to the Master and for all good work." For whoever wants to purify himself must *previously* have *been* a vessel of dishonor. But of the vessels of mercy, he says clearly that the Lord Himself has prepared them for glory, which he does not say of the damned, who have, and not God, prepared themselves to be vessels of damnation. [613,82]

93. May we conclude from the fact that God punishes sins with sins that God never wanted that those whom He so punishes be saved?

Absolutely not. Much more, it is to be considered diligently, when God punishes sins with sins, that is, punishes those who had been converted, because of their security, unrepentance and willful sins, with hardening and blinding. That should not be taken as if it had never been God's will that such people should come to recognition of the truth and be saved. [613,83]

94. Why must one believe both: as much as God wants to save all people, He wants to harden the obstinate sinners?

This is why: because both are God's revealed will. First, that God wants to take all who repent and believe in Christ into His grace; on the other hand, that He also wills that those who turn willfully away from the holy commandment and turn back to the filth of the world (2 Peter 2:20), decorate their hearts for Satan (Luke 11:25 ff.), and have held the Holy Ghost in contempt (Heb. 10:29) be punished, and since they persist in that, be hardened, blinded and eternally damned. [614,83]

95. What, then, was NOT[21] the cause that Pharaoh was lost?

Pharaoh, of whom it is written in Ex. 9:16 and Rom. 9:17: "I have

---

[21] Emphasis added to prevent confusion. Where emphasis is in italics, it is in the original.

aroused thee exactly so that My power may appear in thee and My name may be proclaimed in all lands." was not destroyed because God supposedly did not wish him to be saved or that He was pleased to will that he should be damned and lost; for God "desireth not that anyone should be lost[22]; also, hath no pleasure in the death of a sinner, but wants that he convert and live." Ezek. 33:11. [614,84]

96. But where does it come from, that God hardened Pharaoh's heart, namely that Pharaoh constantly sins further and further, and the more he is warned, the more hardened he becomes?

That is a punishment of his previous sins and horrible tyranny, which he exercised on the children of Israel much and in many ways, inhumanly and against the accusation of his own heart. [614,85]

97. But why did God finally withdraw His hand from Pharaoh?

Because God had His Word preached and His will proclaimed to him, yet Pharaoh willfully pushed directly against all admonition and warning, then God withdrew His hand from him, and thus his heart was hardened and stiffened, and God showed His judgment upon him; for he did not deserve anything but the fire of hell. [614,85]

98. To what end alone does the holy Apostle introduce the example of Pharaoh in Rom. 9?

For no other reason than to demonstrate the justice of God, which He shows on the unrepentant and despisers of His Word. [614,86]

99. In which way is it in no way meant nor understood, when the Apostle in Rom. 9 introduces the example of Pharaoh?

This is in no way meant or understood, that God begrudged Pharaoh or some other person salvation, but thus ordered in His secret counsel that he should not be able to or want to be saved. [614,86]

100. Why then can we believe with certainty that the doctrine of election, as it is explained here, is the right, Godly teaching of this article?

This is why: for through this teaching and explanation of the

---

[22] 2 Pet. 3:9.

eternal and *saving* election of the chosen children of God *God is given His honor entirely and completely.* [614,87]

101. Why is God given His entire and complete glory through this doctrine?

This is why: because by it is taught that God, out of pure mercy in Christ, without any of our merit or good works, saves us according to the purpose of His will. [614,87]

102. Does the holy Scripture also teach, then, that God saves us solely out of His mercy in Christ according to the purpose of His will?

Yes; for it is written in Eph. 1:5 ff.: "He has ordained us to be His own children, through Jesus Christ, according to the pleasure of His will to the praise of His glory and grace, through which He has made us pleasing in the beloved."

103. So is it the right teaching, if one teaches that there is also a cause of our election by God within ourselves?

Far from it! Further, it is false and not right, when it is taught that not *only* the mercy of God and most holy merit of Christ, but *also in us there is a cause* of God's election, for the sake of which God has elected us to eternal life.

104. How do you prove that there is within us no cause of election?

I prove this thus: for not only *before we had done anything good*, but also *before we were born*, God has elected us in Christ, yes, before the foundation of the world was laid; and "that the purpose of God exists according to His election, it was said to her[23], not by the merits of works but by the grace of the one calling, thus: The greatest shall serve the lesser," Rom. 9:11, ff.; Gen. 25:23. As is written of it: "I have loved Jacob; but Esau have I hated," Rom. 9:13; Mal. 1:2,3. [614,88]

105. But when does this teaching of election give no one cause either to despair or to an insolent, wild life?

When the people are taught that they should *seek* eternal election in *Christ* and His holy *Gospel*, as in the book of life, which excludes no repentant sinner, but draws and calls all poor, burdened and distressed sinners to repentance and recognition of their sins and to faith in Christ, and promises them the Holy Ghost to sanc-

---

[23] Rebekah. For whatever reason, the German text of the FC, which Walther follows, has "to him"; yet Luther's Bible has "zu ihr"—to her, which is how it appears in all English translations, and the Greek text has "auth"— "to her."

tification and renewal. [615,89]

106. What source of comfort, then, does this doctrine give to distressed, afflicted people?

The most *lasting*; namely hat they know *that their salvation is not in their own hand* (otherwise they would lose it much more easily, as happened to Adam and Eve in Paradise, every hour and moment), *but in the gracious election of God*, which He revealed to us in Christ, *out of Whose hand no one will rip us.* John 10:28; 2 Tim. 2:19 [615,90]

107. Who teaches certainly and without any doubt a false doctrine of election?

Those who so teach the doctrine of the gracious election of God that distressed Christians cannot console themselves with it, but instead are caused thereby to despair, or the unrepentant are strengthened in their willfulness. In that way, it is doubtless certain and true that that doctrine is not according to the Word and will of God, but according to reason and driven by the instigation of the pesky devil. [615,91]

108. How do you prove that the doctrine of election is certainly not understood and set forth according to God's Word when it does not give the distressed, afflicted Christian the most lasting comfort?

I prove this by this, that the Apostle testifies in Rom. 15:4: "Everything which is written is written for teaching, that we, through patience and comfort of the Scripture, have hope." Where, however, such comfort and hope is weakened in us or even taken from us through the Scripture, there it is certain that it has been understood and presented contrary to the will and meaning of the holy Ghost. [615,92]

109. Should we Lutherans therefore also remain true and constant with the teaching about election in our dear Confession until death?

Yes. We remain with this simple, right, useful explanation, which has a lasting, good foundation in God's revealed will.

110. What sort of questions and disputations, however, should we Lutherans, when we deal with this doctrine, flee and avoid?

All high and clever questions and disputations? [615,93]

111. What should we Lutherans finally reject and condemn in relation to this doctrine?

Everything that is contrary to these simple, useful explanations. [615,93]

112. What then are the errors with regard to the doctrine of election which our Evangelical Lutheran Church has expressly *rejected*?

When it is taught that God does not wish that all people repent and believe the Gospel.

Likewise, that when God calls us to Himself, that He does not seriously mean that all people should come to Him.

Likewise, that God does not want everyone to be saved, but without regard to their sins, solely of His bare counsel, purpose and will, decreed that they cannot be saved.

Likewise, that not *only* the mercy of God and the most holy merit of Christ, *but that in us there is a cause* of the election of God, for the sake of which God has elected us to eternal life. [500,16-20]

113. What does our church judge about all these errors in regard to the doctrine of election?

It explains: "These are all blasphemous and horrible false teachings, through which all comfort that they have in the holy Gospel and the use of the holy Sacraments is taken from Christians, and therefore should not be tolerated in the church of God." [500,21]

114. But why is the teaching of our evangelical Lutheran Church certainly the right doctrine, revealed by God in His Word, on which we can live and die comforted?

Namely from the two unassailable grounds: For through this short explanation of the eternal election of God, God is given His honor entirely and completely, that He alone, out of pure mercy, without any merit of ours, saves us according to the purpose of His will; besides that, no one is given any reason to despare or to coarse, wild life. [499,15]

Afterword

Before we now take our leave from our beloved readers, may we be allowed, in regard to the use of this little book, to give a few hints.

It is well known that the teaching has become loud, that our dear God has not decided to choose His elect out of the world and decided to make them His children; whereas Christ says it plainly in John 15:19: "I have chosen you from the world, therefore the world hates you." Against that, it is taught that God first saw how people would conduct themselves, which of them would forsake the world and become believing children of God and would remain so to the end, and only in consequence thereof, that God foresaw this, did He elect such people to be His children, to sanctification and to salvation.

Anyone who wants to see sees immediately, however, that it first of all makes no sense when one teaches that God has elected certain people to be His children, to sanctification and to salvation in consequence of His having seen that they would believe to the end—hence already be and become holy and blessed children of God! Yet still those who teach that assert that this doctrine of theirs is not only right, but that it and no other has always been the teaching of our entire Lutheran church. Yes, they say, this doctrine is to be found also in our Lutheran confessional writings, and more exactly in the last general confessional writing, namely in the Formula of Concord!

This, however, rests at best on a dreadful self-deception. Of this, that God has elected certain people to be His children and to salvation in consequence of their foreseen lasting faith, hence in consequence of their foreseen right conduct, there is nothing anywhere in our Lutheran Confessions, not even one little word. In the eleventh article of the Formula of Concord, however it is clearly and definitely the exact opposite—namely the reverse, that election is a cause of our salvation and of all that belongs to the attainment thereof: a cause of faith and conversion, which the Formula of Concord proves from Acts 13:48 and other passages, where it says, "And so many became believers as were of them ordained to eternal life." (See Question 10; cf. Questions 24, 46, and 55.)

Against that, to be sure, the defenders of that false doctrine object as follows: The Formula of Concord, they say, calls election a cause of salvation, and hence also a cause of faith because it takes the word "election" otherwise than as our later Lutheran theologians do, namely in a broader, quite general sense, to which also the general decree of grace belongs, which extends to all people. Yes, they say, this general decree of grace is precisely the chief part of the decree of election! Of course one can neither speak nor think rightly of election other than as one speaks and thinks on the general decree of grace, according to which God wishes to save, or lead all people to salvation, because God has not decided to save the elect in any other way than the way He wants to save all people. But that does not mean that the decree of salvation, which extends to all people, is either election or a part thereof.

Hence, everyone can see here as well that this also makes no sense, to talk of an election if it extends to all people; for an election that extends to all without exception is a nullity, a contradiction within itself. An election shows that not all are taken, but out of all, only some, be it few or many, are chosen. Even a child can see that.

The Formula of Concord also says quite expressly, however, that the eternal election of God, or God's preordaining to salvation, does not extend to the pious and the wicked at the same time, thus not to all people, but only to the children of God, who were elected and ordered to eternal life before the foundation of the world was laid. (See Questions 5 and 6.)

So how can one say that the Formula of Concord teaches an election of grace in a broader sense that extends to all people, to the pious and the wicked? Hence we have already, in the tract, "The Doctrinal Controversy of Election", warned the readers to hold fast to both chief principles (Questions 5-7 and 10-12). We repeat that here. If you do not want to accept any un-Lutheran, un-confessional doctrine, then stand unshakably fast on both of those chief principles of our Confession. Do not let those important, decisive principles be wrested out of your hands, or more important, out of your hearts by any tricky sophistry. Furthermore, keep your distance from all conjurers' tricks through which anyone tries to prove to you that those principles signify something other than what they say.

Therefore read Questions 5-7 and 10-12 in this book, with their answers, attentively; you will soon see that, according to God's Word and our Lutheran Confession, election does not include all people, but only the elect children of God, who have been chosen and ordered to salvation, before the foundation of the world was laid, and that this election of God, which does not extend to both the pious and the wicked, is a cause that shapes, helps, works and promotes our salvation and all that pertains to it, that the gates of hell should not prevail against it.

Do not let yourself be deceived! The Formula of Concord is no such confused writing, that it should first say, election extends only to the elect children of God, and a few lines later say, it extends to all people.

Our opponents, to be sure, rely on the fact that the Formula of Concord itself says, when one wants to consider and speak properly and fruitfully about election, one must put together the entire doctrine of the purpose, will and decree of God concerning our redemption, calling, justification and salvation, as Paul in Rom. 8:29 ff.; therefore, our opponents say, the whole general decree of grace as to all men belongs to election. It remains, however, first, that it would make no sense that the general decree of grace is a part of the decree of election, for Christ says clearly and plainly, "Many are called, but *few* are chosen." But the Formula of Concord also says expressly, that it speaks of *our* redemption, calling, justification and salvation, with which it shows plainly, that it is speaking of all this in relation to the elect, because God does not lead them to salvation by any other way than that by which He wants to lead all people.

That is why the Formula of Concord, to Question 24, also explains that in what came before, where it spoke of the calling, justification, sanctification and perseverance in the Cross, described "the way by which God wants, through His grace, gifts and working thereto", "to bring, help, further, strengthen and preserve them (the elect)." Everything that the Formula of Concord says in Questions 21-23 is thus related to the elect, which is why it also says, at the conclusion, where it is summarized: "That He ultimately has called and justified *those whom He elected*, and also wants to make them eternally blessed and glorious in eternal life."

One also perceives that this is the true sense of our dear Confession in that the Formula of Concord says after question that Paul also handles and explains this article in that way in Rom. 8:29 ff.. But how does Paul handle and explain this article in Rom. 8:29 ff.? Thus, that he to be sure speaks of the calling, justification and glorification, but only in connection with the elect; for he writes thus:

"29 For whom he did foreknow, he also did predestinate to be conformed to the image of his Son, that he might be the firstborn among many brethren.

30 *Moreover whom he did predestinate*, them he also called: and whom he called, them he also justified: and whom he justified, them he also glorified."

Hence Paul also triumphs in the following:

33 Who shall lay any thing to the charge of God's elect? It is God that justifieth.

34 Who is he that condemneth? It is Christ that died, yea rather, that is risen again, who is even at the right hand of God, who also maketh intercession for us.

35 Who shall separate us from the love of Christ? ...

38 For I am persuaded, that neither death, nor life...

39...shall be able to separate us from the love of God, which is in Christ Jesus our Lord. (Rom. 8:33 ff.)

Paul has dealt with the general decree of grace, to the extent that it extends to all people, in the previous chapters, but from the second half of the 8th chapter on, he now speaks of this decree in relation to the elect. Therefore, to seek to prove from what the Formula of Concord says to Questions 20-23 that the Formula of Concord speaks of a gracious election in a broader sense, that extends to all people rests quite obviously on a terrible misunderstanding or on a willful distortion and perversion.

Additionally, the first part of the Formula of Concord, which teaches a short abstract of the doctrine of election, hence should contain precisely the main points of the same, does not contain those 8 points (see Questions 21-23), in which points, according to our opponents, the chief point of the election of grace, namely the general decree of grace, ought to be contained. If our opponents were right, then the first part of the Formula of Concord omitted the very chief point! But there is a good explanation for that. The Formula of Concord did not omit that which is for it the main point, but rather our opponents want to smuggle what they think is the main point into it. But the general decree of grace is, to be sure, the chief point of the whole Christian doctrine, but not the chief point, yes, not a part of election.

But they say, "Yes, does not the Formula of Concord, to Question 33, also say expressly that the promise of the Gospel is a general one, and consequently, that it extends to all people?" We answer, "Yes, of course! But where does the Formula of Concord say that this is election? Nowhere! Rather, it treats at this point of this: about what we must 'in all ways hold stiffly and firmly, when we want to consider our eternal election to salvation in a useful way,' namely, if we want to find out whether we belong to those 'who can and should take up this doctrine to their comfort.'" (See Question 27.)

Thus, at this point, we are not dealing with the formation of election, or what it actually is, but rather with what we have to hold firmly if we want to "consider our eternal election to salvation in a useful way." For we can certainly only do that when we first hold this firmly, that God loved all people, and thus also redeemed us, that God calls all people and thus also us to Himself seriously, and that God wishes to bring all people and thus also us to repentance and faith, preserve them to the end in that, and eternally save them. For God has promised no one, that He would reveal to him His election directly. Hence, how could we dare believe, that we ourselves belong to the elect, if we could not first of all hold to the general decree of grace, that extends quite certainly to all people, and thus extends quite certainly to us?

The same is to be said also about another place in the Formula of Concord which many now also distort miserably, in which it says that "God directs all people to Christ as to the book of life, in which they can seek the eternal election of the Father." (See Questions 80-81.) Many now also want to draw from that that the Formula of Concord thus teaches a gracious election of all people. But there can hardly be any more stupid thought than this conclusion and this proof. Should then our confession contradict Christ to His face, who repeatedly says, "Many are called, but *few* are chosen"? (Matt. 20:16; 22:14; cf. 1 Cor. 1:26-28.)

Instead, our Formula of Concord wants to say with these words, as the context shows: "Whoever wants to become certain whether he belongs to the few elect may not speculate about the secret decree of God, or pray and wait until God reveals it to him by an angel or directly through the speaking of the Holy Spirit. Rather, he must seek his election in Christ, who is also his Savior. If he really seeks it there, he will find it, excepting no person. For since God according to His revealed Word has decided from eternity, "he whom He wants to save, He wants to save through Christ," and he whom He has elected, He also wants to call through the Gospel of Christ and, through faith, justify him and make him His child, every person can and should become certain that he is called and stands in a justifying faith, and ascertain by no other way that he belongs to the elect.

From this you can see, dear reader, that these people go around with untruth, against their own better knowledge and conscience, who say that through this doctrine, that election is not to all, the doctrine of the universal grace of God in Christ is obscured, yes, denied! Moreover, the doctrine of election can only be regarded in a useful or comforting manner if before, during and afterwards, the teaching of general grace is also pushed most energetically—which we, by God's grace, do with all faithfulness. From this it does not follow that thus the teaching of general grace belongs to the doctrine of election as a substantial part, yes, as the chief part! It has instead the same explanation as with the doctrine of justification and redemption.

The doctrine of the justification of a poor sinner before God cannot possibly, of course, be presented in a useful way and for the comfort of repentant sinners, if the doctrine of the redemption of all people has not first been established as a foundation; but is thereby the doctrine of the redemption of all people a part, yes, the chief part, of the doctrine of the justification of a poor sinner before God? In no way! It is not a part thereof, but the ground on which it rests.

And in that way, then, the doctrine of the general decree of grace and of election are related. Likewise, the general decree of grace is not a part of election, but is the ground on which it rests. A preacher who were to begin his teaching with the doctrine of election (as indeed the Calvinists really do right at the beginning of their Heidelberg Catechism), would be a terrible distorter of the counsel of God on the salvation of people. The doctrine of general grace is the chief doctrine of all Christendom, with which alone must be the beginning, but must also be continued later and never stopped, if people are to be led to salvation.

The doctrine of election however, does not belong to the first letters of the divine Word, and is not milk like the doctrine of general grace, but is strong food which is for those who have exercised minds about the distinction between good and evil (Heb. 5:12-14). It has only the purpose of giving those who have already become believers a particular comfort, namely the splendid comfort that their salvation does not rest in their hand, from which they could only too easily, for the sake of the world, the flesh and the devil lose it, but in Christ's hand; that God Himself, as He has begun the good work in them, will also carry it out until the day of Jesus Christ; that their salvation is so firmly founded in God's eternal election that even the gates of hell can do nothing against it; that therefore nothing, nothing will rip them out of Christ's hand.

So that you now, dear reader, do not ever let yourself be moved by anything from the pure, Scriptural doctrine of our church on election and to accept the new teaching which many now want to slide in under our Formula of Concord, we want to bring your attention on three more points.

The first of these three points is this:

Our dear Formula of Concord rejects most decisively the error of the Synergists, that not God's mercy and the most holy merit of Christ alone, but *also in us* is a cause of the eternal election of God, for the sake of which God has elected us to eternal life. (See Question 113, cf. Also Questions 87, 101-105.) After this is the teaching that also the foreseen faith is a cause of election, beyond all doubt an un-Lutheran, synergistic doctrine, because faith is something which is not in God but *in us*. Perhaps you will say here, "What? Is faith, then, according to the Formula of Concord, not necessary to be one of the elect? Moreover, according to the express declaration of the Formula of Concord, are not the faithful, pious children of God alone the elect? (See Questions 5, 45.) Yes, of course faith is very simply necessary if a person is to be justified before God and saved; for the Holy Scripture says with clear words: "Without faith, it's[24] impossible to please God." (Heb. 11:6) "Lord, thine eyes look for faith." (Jer. 5:3)[25] "Whoever does not believe will be damned." (Mark 16:16)

---

[24] The contraction is in the German; the translator is aware that ordinarily one would not use a contraction in a Bible quotation.
[25] ESV: "look for truth?"; KJV: "are not thine eyes upon the truth?"

"Whoever does not believe is already judged." (John 3:18) "Whoever does not believe the Son will not see life, but the wrath of God remains over him." (John 3:36) But it does not follow from this that God chose the elect only when He foresaw that they would believe to the end; instead, only this follows, that God certainly could not have elected anyone to be His child and to salvation if He had not at the same time decided to bring him Himself through His grace to faith, and to preserve him in faith until the end. And that God has already ordained the elect thereto is exactly the clear teaching of the Formula of Concord. (See Questions 10, 24, 46, 55.)

That is not a sort of Calvinistic teaching, but the pure Lutheran doctrine. The malicious Calvinists teach namely that God has absolutely, that is, entirely unconditionally, elected, from His bare favor, not moved through Christ's merit, but our deal Lutheran church teaches, God elected for the sake of Christ's merit and through faith in Christ, which He decided at the same time to give. Thus, it is not, according to God's Word and our Confession, that God elected because God foresaw that the elect would conduct himself rightly, let himself be drawn into the order of grace, namely let faith work in himself, or even, he will decide for Christ on his own, like the Iowans say, and cooperate in working faith; but because God has, out of bare mercy for the sake of Christ, ordained, to bring him to Christ, to keep him in faith until the end, and to save him eternally in this and no other way. (See Questions 10, 24, 46, 55.)

The elect have therefore done nothing at all toward their own election, and hence can therefore ascribe nothing to themselves relating to the work of their salvation, not even the least. So note that well, dear reader! For only then, when you make only God's mercy and Christ's merit the cause of His election to be His child and to salvation, do you give to God alone, completely and fully, the glory of your salvation. (Cf. Questions 95 and 115.) But woe to you, when you take this honor from God and Christ and ascribe it, even a part of it, to yourself! That is the most frightful idolatry which you can commit, and the certain way to damnation. (See Questions 113 and 114.)

For Christ will not let this glory be taken from Him; hence He says, "You have made work for Me in your sins, and have made exertion for Me in your misdeeds. I erase your transgressions for my own sake, and do not remember your sins." (Is. 43:24-25)[26] Woe to him who diminishes this honor to Christ! He will reject him, and with him, his salvation.

To be sure, our opponents say that they would also concede that

---

[26] The German is in the present tense. ESV puts the second sentence into the future tense; KJV has "blotted out" in the present but has "will not remember thy sins."

faith is solely God's work of grace in the believer; if then they taught that election happened in consequence of foreseen persevering faith, then they would in no way deny that election is entirely of the grace of God and not to be ascribed to the cooperation and the merit of the person. Only because they at the same time insist on it, it would be false that the elect are not chosen with consideration of their "conduct", one would have to teach that one is elect in consideration, in consequence, under the condition of faith.

Thus one sees from this that our opponents are not serious when they concede that faith is purely God's work of faith in the believer; otherwise they would not reject and damn the teaching that faith is not the cause of election, but the other way around, that election is the cause of faith. If they were persuaded in their hearts that faith is solely God's free gift of grace, they would also believe that God decided from eternity to give the elect, who will all believe until the end, this faith. From that, that they turn faith into a condition of election, which must be fulfilled from the side of the person, unfortunately they give it clearly to be understood that they see faith (perhaps many without really conscious of it) as something that a person must and does render, not as something which God gives to the person and has decided to give him from eternity.

Martin Chemnitz, the chief composer of the Formula of Concord, therefore writes very nicely as follows:

> It doesn't have the meaning that God alone prepares salvation, but people who want to be saved would and could seek for themselves how to attain that. Rather, God has considered each and every person of the elect who should be saved through Christ in His eternal counsel, and has prepared and elected them for salvation, and also ordained how *He* wishes to bring them to that, assist them and preserve them through His grace, gifts and working.

Soon thereafter, Chemnitz continues thus: "So God's Election does not *follow after* our *faith* and righteousness, but *goes before* as a *cause* of all that; for those whom He has ordained and elected, He has also called and made righteous (Rom. 8)." (See Chemnitz's "Handbook" from the year 1574.)

According to this, all those who reject the doctrine that faith follows election and that election goes before faith as its cause, for the sake of honesty ought at least admit that they in no way are fighting only against Missouri (as they have until now pretended), but also against Chemnitz and against the Formula of Concord composed by him. If they are still able to deceive many that he means that their teaching is the teaching of Chemnitz and of the Formula of Concord, sooner or later it will become evident to everyone that they have spoken untruth with their pretense.

By the way, those among our opponents who are really no synergists or Semipelagians who ascribe a cooperation in the work of their salvation and who, without noticing it, have wandered into a synergistic and semipelagian doctrine—they should come through this to the recognition that all synergists, all Semipelagians, yes, all rationalists now place themselves on their side against us and cheer them on. For God's sake, they should not think that because they have such a big following for themselves and we so few for us, they must represent the truth, and that we are, on the other hand, in error.

We now live in the age of synergism. Not only almost all sects that claim to be faithful, but also almost all Lutherans claiming to be faithful are now stuck in synergism (forgive us this expression!) up to their ears. We therefore do not doubt for a moment that God has permitted that a restless spirit has stirred up the present dispute over the doctrine of election because God will at least soon cleanse His orthodox Church from the highly dangerous and contaminating leaven of synergism. Woe to them who remain standing on the side of those who fight against God in this dispute!

Many upright men may perhaps do it because they think our opponents stand on the side of many old faithful theologians; hence they hold to our opponents only out of respect for and in trust of these theologians. It will, however, soon become apparent that our opponents not only do not only disagree with the Formula of Concord but with those theologians, but have brought up a teaching precisely of the Crypto-Calvinists (which they call us) against whom the Formula of Concord was issued in the year 1577.

The second of the three points which we feel compelled to bring to our readers' attention is this:

Our dear Formula of Concord teaches according to God's Word: Since our salvation can easily be lost through the weakness and wickedness of our flesh, or through trickery and violence of the devil and the world be ripped out of our hands, God has (*indistinct in text*) to guard our salvation well and certainly, *ordained* in His eternal decree, which cannot fail or be overthrown, and laid in the hand of our Savior Jesus Christ, out of which no one can rip us, to keep safely. Hence Paul also, in Rom. 8:28,39, calls out with all elect: "Because we are called by the decree, who will separate us from the love of God in Christ?" (See Questions 56 and 107.)

Now, however, our opponents teach, that salvation of faithful Christians is certain from the side of God, for from His side, God does everything that He can that faithful Christians persevere and be saved; but because even faithful Christians still have weak, wicked flesh, they must be uncertain of their salvation, and it is only an evil deception if they think they are certain of it. Of course our opponents can according to their doctrine not conclude otherwise, since they make the certainty dependent on what the person does. For they say, a person does not persevere in the faith because God has ordained and elected him from eternity to be His child and to salvation, but only under the condition that a person persevere and go the way to salvation until the end, and because God has foreseen that a person would remain true until death, He has elected him also to salvation.

Now no faithful Christian can deny, they say, that he will perhaps fall away and lose faith, for the sake of the weakness and wickedness of his flesh and the trickery and violence of the world and Satan; thus even a faithful Christian cannot be certain of his salvation until he is already in his last moments. Against that the Formula of Concord teaches that God, precisely because of the weakness and wickedness of the fleash and because of the trickery and violence of the devil and the world, has taken the salvation of the faithful into His hand through election, so that the faithful would know that nothing, neither in the world, nor in hell, neither flesh, nor world, nor Satan.

Our opponents however teach the exact opposite. According to them, the weakness and wickedness of the flesh makes the election of faithful Christians, and thus their salvation, uncertain, while according to our Confession election should serve precisely that purpose, that faithful Christians can and should be certain of their salvation despite flesh, world and devil; their salvation, we say, as our confession expressly witnesses, "because only the elect are saved." (See Question 28.)

With their new teaching of election, our opponents go so far, and must go so far, as to assert that, in distress, election of course gives no comfort, or only when the person has a firm, certain, strong, joyful faith, and is therefore of good hope that he will, with God's help in faith, overcome everything. Our Formula of Concord, however, teaches the opposite, namely that precisely in distress, when a person sees absolutely nothing good in himself, feels no faith in himself, and when all other comfort vanishes, election gives him the "most enduring comfort of all"; yes, that a person in distress, exactly when doubts in his perseverance and salvation arise in him, learns for the first time how comforting election is, for this teaches him that his salvation does not stand in his hand, but in the gracious election of God. (See Questions 107, 38.) This reason by itself shows incontrovertibly that our opponents teach an entirely different election from what our church in its Confession, from which they have obviously shamefullly fallen away.

The third of the three points which we especially feel compelled to bring to our readers' attention is finally the following:

Our dear Formula of Concord teaches, with Luther, that a person who wants to be saved, must first concern himself with Christ and His Gospel, that he recognize his sin and Christ's grace, and after that struggle with sin, and after that, when he comes into distress under cross and suffering, predestination or election will teach him how useful and comforting it is. (See Question 38.)

Now, however, our opponents teach, election is nothing other and nothing further than the decision of God to regard the faithful and to save them in consequence of their foreseen faith, persevering to the end. Hence that is quite obviously a completely different doctrine of election from that of the Formula of Concord, for a person does not learn that the "election" that our opponents teach is "useful and comforting" for the first time when "he is under distress under cross and suffering." What our opponents call "election" is nothing further than a main part of the general divine decree of grace, namely that God already decided from eternity to save all those who live and die in faith. That is not something to be preached and considered only when Christians come into "distress under cross and suffering." Rather, that belongs, as it is said in the Epistle to the Hebrews, to the "first letters of God's words," to the "milk" for young children, to the "teaching from the beginning of Christian life," (Heb. 5:12-13; 6:1), through which people are first brought to belief and a Christian life.

See, dear reader, if you take the doctrine of our opponents and test it, you will find that it simply does not fit anywhere with what the Formula of Concord says about election. That is however an incontrovertible sign that the doctrine of our opponents is an entirely different one. Otherwise it would naturally, even if presented in different words, fit with at least the sense of everything that the Formula of Concord says about election. But if you pay attention properly, you will more and more figure out that our opponents really teach absolutely no election at all, but only call "election" something that is nothing further than the general decree of grace, or only the last part of the same.

But you must not, dear reader, let yourself be taken in by the bold way in which our opponents come forward, just become more brazen, and the more we lay out proofs against them from Scripture and Confessions, instead of testing them, or quietly opposing them, simply continue to shout, "You are Calvinists! Yes, you are Calvinists!" But that has always been the way of false teachers, that when they did not know any more proofs that they could bring forward, they just repeated all the more shamelessly their old assertions, power plays and accusations, and only then turned out to be really agitated, ardent and fanatical, naturally in the hope that they thereby could in part motivate their comrades, and in part win over the thoughtless crowd to themselves.

Still, we must now hurry to finish, so that this little book does not become all too long.

Finally, may it be permitted to us to add the following few words.

Dear reader, do you already stand in faith, or not? If you do not stand in faith, then I must once more advise you, as already in the foreword: Do not concern yourself at all right now with the secret-filled doctrine of election! In this your present unbelieving condition, you need someone to teach you the first letters of the divine words. The doctrine of repentance and conversion is what you need.

But if you are already, through God's grace, in a living faith, then let me ask you further: Did you give yourself your faith in some way? You will say, "Oh, no, I couldn't have done the slightest that I come to a living faith through the Word of the Gospel, and I did not come to the Word, but the Word came to me." "Well! But do you maybe mean that you thus came to faith only accidentally?" Doubtless, you will answer that, "Oh, no; if I thought that, I would have to be a pure heathen; nothing just sort of happens."

All right, then let me ask you further, "Whom have you to thank, that you have come to faith through the Word of God?" You say, "I can thank only the mercy of God and the most holy merits of Christ for that. It was God who opened my hard, closed heart, as once with Lydia, that I thereupon paid attention to what I read and heard from God's Word. I really did not earn this with anything! Because of my many sins, I would have deserved much more that God would neither call me nor bring me to faith, but rather that He would let me die and rot in my sins. My conversion is a mystery to me, myself. I only know this much, that I did nothing for it."

"Do you mean, then, that God first thought in time of bringing you to faith? Only then, when your eyes opened, as you now recognized the misery of your sin and God's grace in Christ, came to faith, and became a different person?" You will say, "How could I mean that? For I know from God's Word that God not only foreknew but decided in advance in eternity all the good that He does in time."

So then let me ask you only one more thing: "Do you also hope to be saved?" You will answer, "Yes, I hope that. If I did not hope that, I would have to reject Luther's 'Christian Questions'; then I could not once say with the whole Christian Church in firm faith the third article, in which it says, 'I believe ...an eternal life,'[27] and not say with our Catechism, 'I believe... that God will give me, together with all believers in Christ, an eternal life. This is most certainly true.'

[27]Translated as it appears in the German text; this is the phrase we know in English as "the life everlasting."

"And my dear Lord Jesus Christ says, "My sheep hear my voice, and I know them and they follow me; and I give them eternal life; and they will never die, and no one will rip them out of my hand." (John 10:27-28.) How then could I doubt my salvation?"

Rightly so, dear reader! See, then you have there in very short words, the whole doctrine of election as a summary. For that and nothing else is what the Formula of Concord teaches about election and what we teach with it, and that confession of ours, and we with it, reject whatever does not agree with this simple teaching. So if you become confused in the many disputations that are now raised over the doctrine of election, just be comforted! If you stay with that simple belief, then you have the right doctrine of election, even if you have never yet in your life heard anything about the word "election." In this belief, do not let yourself be made crazy by anything! Let those who cannot put it aside or who because of their vocation to the defense of the truth must do it argue over the doctrine of election and its secrets. You however, stay with that little saying, in which God the Lord Himself says, "Israel, you bring yourself into misfortune; for your salvation is only in me." (Hos.13:9.)[28] Do not deviate from this golden saying either to the right or to the left, and you will be on the right road, and the end of this, your way of faith, will be eternal salvation.

God the Father, for the sake of Jesus Christ, His only-begotten Son and merciful Savior of all sinners, help us in this through the working and governing of the Holy Ghost. To which eternal, triune God be thanks, laud, praise and honor here in time and from the mouth of all angels and elect from eternity to eternity. Amen.

---

[28] See note 8.

www.ingramcontent.com/pod-product-compliance
Lightning Source LLC
Chambersburg PA
CBHW071929290426
44110CB00013B/1537